"The worst disaster and largest capitulation of British history"
— British Prime Minister Winston Churchill on the fall of Singapore.

"The fall of Singapore gives the well-known back-seat driver a field day."
— United States President Franklin Roosevelt.

"All the talk of war had fallen on deaf ears as we went about our business smug in the knowledge that the British were invincible."
— Former Social Affairs Minister Othman Wok, who was a teenager during the Japanese invasion of Singapore.

"The war years did prove that we are a very resilient people."
— Honorary President of the Chinese Chamber of Commerce Tan Keong Choon.

"What I studied had no application. It would have been better if I had taken a course on how to be streetwise."
— Former Deputy Prime Minister Toh Chin Chye, who was a college student during the Occupation.

"Before the war, you regarded the British, the white man, as a superior race. The Japanese changed all that."
— Novelist Goh Sin Tub.

THE
BAMBOO
FORTRESS

TRUE SINGAPORE
WAR STORIES

By H. SIDHU

ANATIVE Publication

ISBN 981-00-3101-7

To my parents, who lived
through this period.

Acknowledgements

My sincere thanks goes to all who agreed to be interviewed. Without their cooperation, this book would not have been possible. I also wish to thank the Institute of Southeast Asian Studies for granting me access to their research material and Ian Carter of the Imperial War Museum in London for his prompt assistance. Finally, I extend my gratitude to my sister, Anup, for her generous advice and support.

Contents

Contents

Introduction

In 1941, Singapore was one of the four great fortresses of the world, ranking up there with Pearl Harbour, Gibraltar and Malta. But the sinking of the battleships Prince of Wales and Repulse was a blow that Fortress Singapore never recovered from.

War heroine Elizabeth Choy summed up the general feeling in Singapore at the news of the sinking of the ships when she said, "When the Prince of Wales and the Repulse came and both of them were sunk within a short while of their arrival, I was very sad, very depressed. I realised it would be extremely difficult for the British to hold out."

Subsequently, the fate of the ships was to prove a harbinger of the fate of the Fortress.

It is a story worth recollecting before we move on to the Invasion and Occupation of Singapore as told by Singaporeans.

The destroyer Express evacuating sailors from the doomed Prince of Wales

I saw the destroyer alongside beginning to move off, so I ran as fast as I could and jumped out and down.

— Robert Woodhead, a sailor on the HMS Prince of Wales.

The sinking of the Prince of Wales and the Repulse

"In all the war, I never received a more direct shock."

— *War-time British Prime Minister Sir Winston Churchill, on receiving news that the battleships Prince of Wales and Repulse had been sunk by Japanese forces.*

The expensive and much boasted about Singapore Naval Base was ready in time for the war. The only important component missing was the fleet.

The British were thin on naval forces in this region, partly because they expected the Americans to use the base in the event of a Japanese attack. Churchill did, however, send two vaunted British battleships to defend the island and patrol the region. His military advisers argued against his decision but Churchill firmly believed that a small but effective naval force could put the brakes on the Japanese expansion in Southeast Asia.

For their time, the two ships were giants. The Prince of Wales was a spanking new 35,000-ton King George V-class battleship. Incorporating the best and latest technology, including the most recent innovations in radar equipment, the Prince of Wales was considered unsinkable.

Its companion, the battle cruiser, Repulse, however, was already 25 years old by then. Built not long after the First World War, its weaponry was clearly outdated, although the 32,000-ton battle cruiser itself was in good condition.

The British also wanted to send their new aircraft carrier, the Indomitable, but the carrier ran aground in the West Indies, and the battleships proceeded to Singapore without any air cover.

News of their arrival spread fast through the island. With the battleships in dock, the armoury of Fortress Singapore seemed complete. The ships drew large crowds, which, no doubt, included a few spies because when the Japanese pilots took on the two ships they had a ready strategy to take advantage of every weakness.

In the early morning hours of Tuesday, December 8, 1941, the ships left their berth in Singapore. They sailed as part of a flotilla cryptically called, Force Z, under the command of Admiral Sir Tom Phillips, the new Commander-in-Chief of the Eastern Fleet. Four other ships, all destroyers, made up the full complement.

Until today, historians decry the foolhardiness of Phillips' mission to take the battleships to Kota Baru on the east coast of Malaysia without any air cover to attack Japanese vessels that were transporting troops to reinforce Lt- Gen Tomoyuki Yamashita's advance landing party.

Phillips, however, was of the firm view that the spanking new Prince of Wales was unsinkable. He also had a lot of faith in the old Repulse. He expected, in any case, to receive air support from the British bases in the north of Malaya. What Phillips did not know was that the Japanese had by that time wiped out the air defence of northern Malaya. When news arrived that the Japanese had overrun the air bases, the ships had already sailed out of port and Phillips was not inclined to turn them back.

As the six ships sailed on the high waters up the east coast of Malaya with no air cover, they were, by all the wisdom of the military textbooks, sitting ducks for the Japanese forces. If Phillips consoled himself with the conventional wisdom that no battleship could be sunk by an air attack alone, he was to be proven wrong.

The Japanese vessels that Phillips had so boldly ventured to attack were indeed a plum target. Twenty-eight troop transport vessels were accompanied by only two battleships under the command of Vice-Admiral Takeo Kurita. However, they also had full air support from the strategic Twenty-second Air Flotilla based at two stations in Vietnam.

When the Japanese heard that British ships were heading their way, their Air Flotilla based in Saigon rushed out reconnaissance planes to locate them. Although he was not aware of how close he got to his target, Phillips was actually within 15 miles of the Japanese troop ships before he was spotted at 11.30 am on Wednesday morning by three Japanese pilots. A Japanese submarine, the I-65, also picked up the ships' trail.

Over at the Saigon base, the pilots and ground crew were making preparations in the afternoon for yet another round of their overnight attacks on Singapore when the report of the sighting came in. Immediately the word went out: take out all bombs, refit the planes with 500-pound torpedoes, find the British ships and sink them.

The necessary was done in double quick time and the planes roared off the tarmac at 6 pm, heading straight for the open sea. As the sun set, they began their search for the six British ships. The Japanese pilots had heard of the reputation of the Prince of Wales and were keen to bag the trophy.

But they were not to locate their prey that easily. Low on fuel from a prolonged search, the fighters and bombers finally returned to base, their torpedoes intact, their guns cold.

Phillips had turned the ships back towards Singapore. Having lost the element of surprise and with no idea of how close he was to his quarry, he decided to return to the safety of Fortress Singapore.

It was 2.30 am. The captain of the Japanese submarine I-58 could not believe his luck as he peered through the periscope. There they were, completely oblivious to his presence, the battleships the British blew their trumpets about.

The captain ordered everyone to battle stations, and prepared his sights. Slowly the ships moved into the crosswires. As the first ship slipped into the bull's-eye, he ordered the torpedoes fired in rapid succession.

Five torpedoes shot out of the belly of the iron shark.

Every one of them missed.

Completely unaware of their razor thin brush with death in the deadly night waters, the British ships continued on their way innocently, while a Japanese submarine captain cursed and swore. He wondered how he was going to report the incident.

Force Z was halfway back to Singapore when Phillips received a report that the Japanese were attempting a landing at Kuantan. He immediately ordered a detour and the fighting ships rushed back northwards to their target, reaching Kuantan at dawn only to find that they had been misled. There was no action there.

Then Phillips received a report that someone had spotted a tug north of his position. He ordered the flotilla to chase up that lead. Without air cover and having already been spotted by the enemy who was presumably on their trail, they were once again heading away from Singapore and its air bases.

When Japanese Commander-in-Chief Admiral Nobutake Kondo heard that the British were heading back north, he ordered every available plane back into the air to take out the Prince of Wales and its companion. His own battle fleet headed south for the confrontation.

The British flotilla, which had gone hunting for troop ships without air cover, was now heading speedily towards a potent force of planes and ships that were hungry to do battle and fully prepared for it.

This time the Japanese pilots came prepared with packed lunches of rice cakes and coffee as they took up a standard search pattern. They hoped that they were not out on another wild goose chase. But as the morning dragged on and the needle on the fuel gauges dipped past the halfway mark, it began to look like it.

Frustrated, and running low on fuel, some pilots gave up the search and started returning to base.

It was 11 am, December 10 when Ensign Hoashi blinked hard and peered again through the glass window at the water below him. Yes, there they were. The Prince of Wales and the Repulse! He had found them! His hand shaking, Hoashi grabbed the microphone and shouted the coordinates of the ships into it.

The ships were about seventy nautical miles southeast of Kuantan at this point. With the confirmed sighting, thirty-four high-level Mitsubishi bombers shot out of Vietnam for their targets. Commonly known as Nells, each was fitted with two 500-pound bombs. Immediately after them, another fifty-two twin-engined torpedo-bombers screamed off the tarmac.

"It is the golden opportunity of a thousand years," the commanding officer said. "Let us use up all our strength."

One of the pilots, Lieutenant Sadao Takai, recalled their deadly strategy. They knew that the Prince of Wales' distinctive feature was her destructive anti-aircraft power. When all her guns fired, 60,000 bullets and shells shot into the air every minute. But they had also received information that the ship's anti-aircraft guns were aimed only for planes which flew above a certain height. The Japanese strategy was to fly below this line of fire. It looked suicidal but it was to prove effective.

Lieutenant Yoshimi Shirai led the first attack. Although the Prince of Wales was nearer to his planes, he aimed for the Repulse instead, perhaps because he knew the older ship was poorly armed. He planned a steady approach towards the Repulse, but with a crafty twist — they would fly over the Prince of Wales on the way, misleading their enemy as to their real target.

The moment the planes were spotted, Phillips ordered all the ships to turn to the right by thirty degrees so that they would point towards the planes, exposing less area as a target. The order went out by flag signal as the admiral did not want to risk using the radio.

On the Prince of Wales, unaware of the enemy's real target, Lieutenant E. J. Kempson watched Shirai's eight planes approach in tight formation. This was the moment of crisis he had been trained for so many years to handle. Kempson barked his sightings into the microphone to the High-Angle Plotting Table, a group of officers below decks who helped plan the ship's response.

"Range 16,500 yards. Height 10,000 feet. Speed 200. Commence! Commence! Commence!"

The officers below decks quickly worked out the correct settings for the ship's 5.25-inch guns and rushed them to the turrets, where the gunners set the fuses to the latest calculations. Kempson kept an eye on the panel before him as the lights came on one by one to indicate which guns were loaded and ready to fire. When all the guns were ready, there was a hooting signal.

But Kempson did not fire straight away. He watched and waited as the Japanese planes approached in a simple, tight formation, lined up like targets in a shooting gallery. They were not moving sideways; they were coming straight on at a steady height and speed. From where he was standing, they looked like sitting ducks. He waited, his finger poised above the red firing button, until the planes reached approximately 12,000 yards. Then he jabbed at the button.

The guns exploded with a deafening roar. They were joined by the thunder of the four-inch guns.

As Kempson watched in disbelief, the planes continued unscathed towards their target. Not one of them was hit. All the shells from the Prince of Wales exploded harmlessly to the right of the planes.

Over in the Repulse, sub-lieutenant G. H. Peters was having the same problem. He corrected his aim more to the left and again the same thing happened — the shells exploded harmlessly to the right of the approaching planes.

The officers on both battleships soon realised what the problem was. Their calculations had not taken into account the fact that their ships were turning to the right by thirty degrees on the admiral's orders. Every time they targetted the planes, the ships moved and ruined their aim. Soon, they had to stop firing on the approaching planes because the guns had veered left so much that they were pointing at their own ships. In fact, the ships had turned so much to the right that now the guns on the left-hand side of the ships began firing off a few rounds at the enemy.

The admiral realised too late what was happening. He quickly gave the order to swerve left by fifty degrees. Precious time was wasted on this second manoeuvre, with the planes getting closer all the time. Now the guns on the left had to stop shooting because the body of the ships got in the way. There were a couple of minutes when none of the guns had the planes in view and could not fire. Meanwhile, Shirai's squadron drew closer with their deadly payload. By the time the guns on the right had the planes in sight, the Japanese pilots had completed their run.

The crew of the Prince of Wales held their breath as the planes soared almost overhead. They could actually see the bombs attached to the belly of the planes. But, miraculously it seemed, the bombs remained attached as the planes roared over their heads. It was only then that the pilots' intentions became clear.

They were headed for the Repulse.

The Repulse crew fired at the planes with everything they had, but there was nothing they could do to take evasive action in the few seconds that the planes took to close the distance. They watched helplessly as each plane dropped one of the two bombs it carried before screaming away in a sharp ascent.

One bomb missed the ship and fell into the water to the right, sending a huge saline spray into the air. Six bombs fell into the water on the left.

But one bomb hit the ship. It smashed through two

floors and exploded on the third level, the armoured deck. Several crew died in that blast and several more were wounded. The ship itself, however, was not seriously damaged.

The men of the Prince of Wales cheered when they saw the Repulse come out of the rain of bombs with minimum damage. But their cheers died on their lips as, within seconds, another formation of planes appeared with torpedoes, coming in low to launch their deadly missiles.

The Prince of Wales fired round after round at the approaching planes but could not hit its targets. The crew watched as the torpedoes detached themselves from the planes when they were about 1,000 yards away. The missiles sank to about twenty feet in the water and cruised steadily towards the ship, their propellers churning up a stream of bubbles to the surface.

Captain Aylwin on the Prince of Wales said, "We watched the approach of nine torpedoes with bated breath. Suddenly there was the most terrific jolt, accompanied by a loud explosion immediately where I was standing on the port side. A vast column of water and smoke shot into the air to a height of about 200 feet, drenching the quarterdeck, and a vast shudder shook the ship. At least one torpedo had hit us."

That torpedo punched a hole about one foot across on the left of the ship, towards the stern, triggering off 330 pounds of explosives on the ship and wrecking at least one of the four propeller shafts.

A crew member said, "The ship appeared to be on

springs; it lifted into the air and settled down again."

Yet another said, "She seemed to bounce three or four times before she steadied herself."

But the most graphic description of all was from a crew member who said there was a sensation similar to "a boy running with a stick along a stretch of corrugated iron, although much magnified".

After about half-a-minute the sensation stopped, but the ship rapidly took in water and began losing speed. Some estimates say the ship took in more than 2,000 tons of water in the first five minutes after the hit. The outer propeller shaft on the left was bent from the force of the explosion and wreaked havoc on the ship as it continued to run. The severe vibration ripped fuel lines apart. The electricity started to fail. In parts of the ship, there were no lights and no ventilation. Communications was affected in several places and without electrical power many guns went out of action.

The Prince of Wales had been dealt a mortal blow.

Men who could see the admiral and captain's faces said they looked stunned and said little. It had taken but six minutes for the Japanese to cripple this battle cruiser. Only five of the Japanese planes had taken direct hits; two of them had to head back to Saigon.

Meanwhile, in the air, the two formations of torpedo bombers circled the ships "like Red Indians about to attack wagons". Lieutenant Sadao Takai, who was leading one of the formations, took his time to assess the situation. He could see that the Prince of Wales was badly damaged. It was moving slower and the stern was just two feet above sea level.

For twelve minutes after the attack on the Prince of Wales, the planes continued to circle menacingly. Then Sadao gave the signal and his formation moved in for the kill — on the Repulse.

He said, "I was starting to shake from the excitement of the moment. The Repulse had already started taking evasive action and was making a hard turn to the right. The target angle was becoming smaller and smaller as the bow of the vessel swung gradually in my direction..."

Tennant continued the hard swing to the right. His ship was about one mile to the south of the Prince of Wales now. He ordered all guns to fire but the planes were coming in too low to be hit.

The captain had another worry. "The torpedoes were not the only hazard, because a small formation of high-level bombers carried out a bombing attack from 12,000 feet at the very moment when the torpedo bombers were making their run."

From Sadao's view, "The air was filled with white smoke, bursting shells and the tracers of anti-aircraft guns and machine guns. As if pushed down by the fierce barrage thrown up by the enemy, I descended to just above the water's surface. The airspeed indicator registered more than 200 mph.

"I do not remember how I was flying the aircraft, how I was aiming and what distance we were from the ship when I dropped the torpedo. In the excitement of the

22

attack, I acted almost subconsciously, my long months of training taking over my actions."

On the Repulse, Tennant took immediate evasive action. Based on the reports that came in continuously, he ordered the ship to make manoeuvres that strained the very iron on the old battleship.

"The whole ship shuddered with the effect of twisting to port and starboard," said Leading Seaman John Robson, who was at the wheel.

He described the scene vividly, "The conning tower filled rapidly with officers and ratings. I was not relieved at the wheel. The noise was terrific when the guns fired. I remember the Quartermaster only a foot away shouting the wheel orders to me, his face red with the effort to be heard above the noise all around us."

Contributing to the din was the deadly rat-a-tat of the machine guns from the planes, aimed at the side of the ship in an attempt to draw blood even as they raced away.

Reginald Jefferies, the Ordnance Artificer, had a close call on that deadly run. He said, "I was passing ammunition to one of the four-inch guns when the Japs came along. Flying just above water level, they aimed their machine-gun fire at us. The chap next to me took a bullet right through his leg and fell.

"When I bent over him to see what I could do for him, they machine-gunned me. A bullet went through my trouser leg, taking a piece out of my trousers. Had this bullet hit my leg, I could never have made it. That was my special bit of luck."

Meanwhile, Tennant did very well. He guided the ship through the path of oncoming torpedoes with the skill of the fishes and the luck of the devil. He estimated that they avoided twelve torpedoes.

The Japanese planes disappeared into the clouds and after the pandemonium of the battle, the sound of the ship cutting through the calm blue sea seemed eerily quiet.

Tennant looked out over the water at the Prince of Wales. She was not sinking, but she was certainly out of commission. Tennant asked his signals officer if the flagship had sent off any distress signals to Singapore, and was told there were none. It was two minutes to noon. Puzzled and angry, Tennant authorised a distress signal from the Repulse. It said, "From Repulse to any British Man of War. Enemy aircraft bombing. My position 134 NYTW 22+09."

At four minutes past noon, Kranji Naval Signal Station in Singapore decoded the message. It took another fifteen minutes to relay it to the Air Headquarters in Sime Road. Minutes later, the Australian 453 Squadron took off. Eleven Brewster Buffaloes flew at maximum speed to rescue the flotilla. But it would take them a full hour to reach the battle scene.

At ten minutes past noon, the Prince of Wales raised two black balls on the signals lines. They were the official signal that the flagship of Force Z was out of control. The battleship was listing to its right and there was no steering control. The Repulse, its crew in relatively high spirits after having successfully avoided nineteen torpedoes in all, moved towards the flagship to offer help. But as it closed the distance to about two miles, a cry went up from a lookout.

The crew rushed to the left of the ship to see what he was pointing at. In the distance they could make out several specks in the sky. Every battle aircraft in the Kanoya Air Corps was heading towards them, closing in for the kill. Their hearts sank. There was no way they were going to survive an attack from twenty-six Bettys. As they watched in despair, the planes split neatly into two groups.

The engine room crew gave the remaining turbines of the Prince of Wales everything they had in a last bid to give the ship enough life to escape. The gunners prepared themselves for what they knew must be the last battle. The ship had taken in too much water to be anything but a sluggish giant, unwilling and unable to respond to orders. This was one fight they would have to stand and face. But it was an uneven fight, and the Japanese pilots knew it.

The pilots assessed the situation quickly. They could see that the Prince of Wales, the pride of the Far Eastern fleet, was the easier target, its stern sitting terribly low in the water. It would require no more than a squadron to sink the flagship, but two squadrons went in for the kill anyway.

A squadron of six Bettys moved into disparate positions to the right of the ship. When they moved in to finish off the listing flagship, they seemed to come from all angles. So confident were the pilots that they came to within 500 yards of the ship to drop their torpedoes so there would be no chance of missing their target.

Petty Officer Coles watched a Model 2 torpedo detach from a plane. In an act of desperation, he aimed his Lewis machine gun at the torpedo and tried to hit it before it reached the water. He could not, of course, and neither could he do anything about the plane itself as it flew over his head because the Lewis guns were designed to fire only at other ships and could not be raised high enough to fire at aircraft.

Ten torpedoes were launched against the Prince of Wales. Four blasted into the ship with such force that it seemed to jump sideways by several inches.

The first torpedo hit the side of the ship so hard that it blew a hole right through to the other end. The second missile was closer to the centre of the ship and blasted open an oil tank. A tall column of water and oil shot into the air. The third hit caused so much water to wash up onto the ship that it swept a crewman overboard.

The fourth torpedo smashed into the side of the ship near its stern, damaging the A Engine Room. The force of the missile made a propeller shaft bend inwards and jam between the hull and another shaft.

The ship took in another 18,000 tons of water after that attack. Its pumps fought a losing battle and several of them were inoperable because the electricity was cut off. Of the eight dynamos that powered the ship, only two still worked. And out of the flagship's four engines, only one still functioned, prodding the ship along at a slow eight knots.

The Prince of Wales was a sitting duck.

At this point, eight Mitsubishis dropped their bombs from 12,000 feet. Ordnance Seaman W. E. England heard the warning on the bridge. He said, "I thought, Lord, not again! Looking up into a perfectly cloudless sky, high up, very high, we could see eight or ten planes with wings tip to tip. As we watched, something that looked like snowflakes fell from them. We watched fascinated and then I awoke to what was happening: bombs! Falling on us!"

Ordnance Seaman D. F. Wilson watched the attack helplessly on board the flagship. He said, "One large bomb detached from each plane. The planes were in such close formation, at least one bomb would hit the ship. It was inevitable that hundreds of men would be dead in a few seconds."

Phillips and his officers watched anxiously as the bombs fell. Just before the bombs hit the ship, Captain Leach shouted, "Now!" and everybody on the bridge ducked.

Meanwhile, on the deck, Seaman England, thinking quickly, shoved his fellow sailors into a steel cabin and slammed the door shut behind them. He said, "There was a crash of thunder. It took awhile for my ears and senses to come back to normal, but I thought that we must be sinking. I unwrapped somebody's leg from around my neck and managed to get the door open. We spilled onto the deck to behold a scene of desolation, with fire and smoke pouring from air vents."

A 500-pound bomb had exploded in the ship's makeshift hospital where between 200 and 300 wounded and others suffering from exhaustion were resting. It claimed a bloody human toll.

The Prince of Wales stood dead in the water within an eerie bubble of silence in the middle of a war zone. The guns were silent, the engines were dead, the men gaped at the devastation. The stern was sinking rapidly as it listed to its left, the water climbing up the deck as one crewman put it, like "the tide was coming in".

Meanwhile the other twenty Mitsubishis arraigned themselves against the Repulse, which was still relatively unscathed from the previous attack.

Tennant, though, was optimistic. He said, "About three miles away, the Japanese had split up into two formations. I started to swing the ship to starboard. The torpedoes were dropped at a distance of 2,500 yards and it seemed obvious that we would be successful once more in combing their tracks."

Then he realised their subterfuge. "The left-hand formation appeared to be making straight for the Prince of Wales. When these aircraft were a little before the port beam at a distance of 2,000 yards, they turned straight at me and fired their torpedoes.

"It now became obvious that if the torpedoes were aimed straight, the Repulse would most certainly be hit as any alteration of course would have caused me to be hit by the other torpedoes that I was in the process of combing."

The gun crew of the Repulse perforated the air with thousands of bullets, trying to put off the aim of the Mitsubishis, but to no avail. The ship was doing a good twenty-seven knots or so in the path of the first nine torpedoes. It managed to swerve this way and that to Tennant's orders to avoid eight of the underwater missiles on the right-hand side. But the ninth underwater missile on the left could not be avoided.

Tennant described the scene in his typically understated British manner, "One torpedo fired from the port side was obviously going to hit the ship and it was possible to watch its tracks for about a minute-and-a-half before the explosion actually occurred. The ship was hit amidship, port side. The ship withstood the hit well and continued to manoeuvre at about twenty-five knots."

The old battleship was designed to take torpedo hits with a sort of false exterior called the torpedo bulge. When the torpedo explosion filled that side of the ship with water, Commander Dendy, who was in charge of damage control, ordered the flooding of a portion of the ship on the opposite side to compensate for the listing on the left. This way the Repulse managed to retain some control over her movements.

But two minutes later, Tennant had to face the third squadron of nine Mitsubishis led by Iki. The pilot had initially focused on the Prince of Wales as his target but when the first squadron of six planes finished off the flagship, he switched his focus to the Repulse.

This time, the planes lined up on both sides of the

Repulse, giving Tennant little leeway to escape. Once again, they moved swiftly into various positions so that when they attacked, they seemed to be coming from all directions. The guns on the Repulse concentrated only on those planes that looked like they were going to torpedo the ship.

Iki led three Mitsubishis in the attack on the left side of the ship, while another six planes attacked from the right. The three planes closed in on the Repulse. When Iki was about 600 yards from the ship, he discharged his torpedoes and banked sharply, firing away at the ship with his machine guns.

The other two planes flew directly over the ship. The Repulse fired thousands of rounds at them as they swooped low. They were both hit. One exploded into a ball of fire and parts of it crashed into the sea, leaving a big circle of flaming oil on the surface. The second Mitsubishi took a hit in the back setting it ablaze and sending it crashing into the sea.

The crew of the Repulse cheered at their double score, but not for long. The three torpedoes from the planes scored direct hits on the left side of the ship, one of them smashing into the engine room. The other two hit the back of the ship. One of them, the torpedo from Iki's plane, smashed the ship's rudder, making it impossible for the ship to steer. As the ship had been making a turn to the right when this torpedo jammed the rudder, it left the ship making a wide arc.

Meanwhile the torpedoes from the other six

Mitsubishis followed in rapid succession. The first crashed its warhead into a boiler room.

The ship took in water rapidly from the holes opened in its sides by the torpedoes and began to list further and further towards its left.

Tennant knew the end had come.

On a Japanese reconnaissance plane, Hoashi reported the state of the ships to Admiral Matsunaga in Saigon, who came to the same conclusion as Tennant: the ships were in their death throes. The Japanese planes on the scene were low on fuel, so the admiral recalled them. He was satisfied that their mission was accomplished. He cancelled the stand by order to the Nells he had in reserve.

Meanwhile Tennant had a painful order to give. He said, "The order for a commanding officer to make, 'Cease all work below deck,' is an exceedingly difficult one, but knowing the ship's construction, I felt very sure that she could not survive."

It was close to 12.30 in the afternoon when Tennant gave the order every ship's captain hopes he will never have to give in the course of his life. He addressed the crew over the ship's loudspeaker system, ordering all of them on deck, and said, "Prepare to abandon ship. Clear away Carley floats."

The Captain's presence on the bridge had a strong effect on the crew's morale. It firmed their resolve and helped ensure an orderly evacuation of the wounded even as explosions inside the ship made it shiver horribly. Not all the lifeboats could be launched in time, but when the wounded on deck were evacuated, the Captain addressed his gallant crew on a megaphone, telling them, "You've put up a good show. Now look after yourselves, and God bless you all."

Then it became a case of every man for himself. The men had been wearing a basic rubber float around their body for the past twenty-four hours so they knew they would float safely once they got into the water, but they had to avoid the danger of being sucked underwater when the full length of the ship sank. The stern was already sinking, so it was important to avoid that area.

The men rushed to the bow and slid down on its side into the sea. Once they were in the water, they swam away for dear life. Many injured themselves badly in that slide, though. Some hit the ship's keel so hard that they broke their ankles. A few even broke their spines. Many died in those awful minutes, some choking to death from the oil in the water which got into their clothes and weighed them down.

Phillips ordered two destroyers to go alongside the Repulse and pick up survivors before it sank, but they never made it on time.

Reginald Jefferies, who had taken a bullet through his trouser leg earlier, said, "We didn't have anybody come alongside and rescue our crew. We lost a tremendous amount of men because most of them were trapped down below.

"When I jumped into the water, I went down a fair distance and I could see a black cover above me. I burst through the fuel oil and started to swim away from the ship.

"The ship was moving slowly now and gradually rolling over. I joined up with a group and headed towards the horizon where we could see a destroyer. We were black with fuel oil. Our eyes were buried in it. We also swallowed a certain amount of it."

There were several others on the Repulse who were badly wounded and trapped on the sinking ship. Those who escaped say there were men hammering away at armoured hatches, trapped in the deeper parts of the ship, where water was flooding in.

Sixteen-year-old Boy Seaman Heydon was one of those who witnessed the loss of his mates in those last moments. "Being a messenger had taught me all the short cuts around the ship and I scrambled up an escape pipe wide enough to take only one person at a time. Several people were following me by the time I came to the door leading out to B Gun Deck — the door was above me at about forty-five degrees.

"The only way I could reach it was to recruit the aid of the one below me, a personal chum of mine, to give me a push. Unfortunately, having done so, he lost his footing and fell back, taking about a dozen others with him.

"I still have nightmares of the sight of those people falling, never to make it up again. When I slid into the water from the gun deck, I was alone and felt sick at the thought that they had lost their lives to save mine."

When the ship sank, Captain Tennant was pulled underwater. He thought he was a dead man, but then suddenly, he felt his body shoved upwards and he hit the bottom of a lifeboat so hard with his helmeted head that it nearly knocked him unconscious. He heard a voice saying, "Here you are, Sir," and felt himself dragged aboard a Carley float by a crewman.

Eleven minutes after the first torpedo from Iki's squadron hit it, the Repulse keeled over. The bow rose out of the water, the red on the hull gleaming in the afternoon sun. Some of the men who were swimming away turned to witness those final moments of their beloved giant as she slipped into the water. One crewman said, "She went down quite peacefully, as though glad it was all over."

Meanwhile, the destroyer Express courageously came alongside the Prince of Wales to evacuate its crew. Phillips called down to his Fleet Staff below decks and told them, "Look after yourselves." There was no expression on his face as he dismissed the officers on deck. But when most of them were gone, he slumped on a stool and looked quite despondent. Captain Leach and the Admiral's secretary, Captain Simon Beardsworth, were believed to have remained on the bridge with him, although several crewmen later reported that they saw the three men walk down the side of the ship and jump into the water.

Planks and ropes were thrown across the two ships for the more able men to cross. Some of the wounded had already been lifted onto Carley floats and dispatched to the sea, where they would be safer. The men sending their mates onto the sea on the floats recalled the horrible screams of those with burns and open wounds as they came into contact with the salt water.

The sinking Prince of Wales threatened the safety of the destroyer parked alongside. The captain of the Express was forced to give the difficult order to release the cable linking the two ships as planks fell into the water because of the widening gap. Men continued to swing across on the ropes until the cable, which had grown so taut it could not even be released by hand, snapped. Some men tried to jump across. Many fell into the water and died.

The flagship's Engine Room Artificer Robert Woodhead was one of those who decided to try and jump across to the Express when he saw the destroyer pulling away. He said, "I looked over to the side and I was horrified. The oil was thick on the water, some bodies were floating on it. I had no life-belt, but on looking around I saw the destroyer alongside just beginning to move off, so I ran along the decks to a clear space to give myself a run at the empty space where the rails had been. Some fellows there shouted to me not to be foolish as the Express was already under way and I would be under the screws, but I just ran as fast as I could and jumped out and down.

"My heels landed around the side of the Express and I pitched forward onto two chaps, breaking my fall. When I recovered from the fright, I looked up at the

Prince of Wales astern and the first thing I noticed was the group of chaps who had cautioned me not to jump, still standing there."

The Express nearly fell victim itself during its daring rescue manoeuvre. As it pulled away, the Prince of Wales rose underneath the destroyer, nearly causing it to capsize. Several men were tipped into the sea by the sudden roll of the ship, but the destroyer managed to get away with no more damage than a twenty-foot gash in the plating of its hull.

Its crew recalled that as the destroyer pulled away to safety, someone from the Prince of Wales called across, "Anyone want a cheap ship?"

As the flagship rolled over on its left side, the hundreds who were still on board ran over to the right-hand side and jumped into the water or swung in on ropes. As more of the ship's belly rose out of the water, many simply slid down the side of the ship into the water. Lieutenant W. M. Graham looked back as he swam away and thought, "How clean the ship's bottom looks."

The ship continued to roll on its left until it was completely upside down in the water. Petty Officer L. V. Leather had an experience then that many a seaman, no matter how deep the salt in his skin, will never experience: he stood on the bottom of the ship he had once sailed on.

"May I say it is something I will never forget," he said. "I was standing on the bottom — almost fell into a large torpedo hole — and I could see the propellers slowly turning. I had the feeling that I was the only one there, but

I could still hear screams from inside the torpedo hole. As the stern began to disappear, I realised the water would reach me where I was standing, so I swam for it."

As the stern sank into the water, many of those swimming away turned to witness the last moments of their ship. Leading Seaman Basil Elsmore said, "My last memory is of a football pitch — the ship's bottom — with all the players and spectators sliding down to one end."

One sailor saluted the ship as it raised its front off the water and then with a wrenching sound as its innards tore apart, it sank into the water. As the men floated in the water, they heard the drone of more planes, only this time it was the drone of the Brewster Buffaloes from Sembawang. The Japanese planes were long gone by now.

As Commander Hilary Norman swam away from the sinking ship, he saw Phillip's body floating in the water. He considered swimming over to the body to remove a ring or something as a remembrance for Phillip's family but decided it was too macabre a thought.

Phillip's body was never found. The body of his secretary, Beardsworth, also sank out of sight, but Leach's body was recovered later.

The following day, a Japanese unit flew over the bloody battle scene, which was now tranquil, and dropped a large bouquet of flowers on the spot where 830 British seamen had died.

It was the first time in naval history that battleships had been sunk in the ocean by air power alone. The

Japanese lost only three planes in the attack.

The sinking of the Prince of Wales and the Repulse became known as the "Pearl Harbour of Southeast Asia". The consequences were disastrous. Churchill said, "As I turned over and twisted in bed, the full horror of the news sank in upon me. There were no British or American capital ships in the Indian Ocean or the Pacific except the American survivors of Pearl Harbour. Over all this vast expanse of waters, Japan was supreme and we everywhere were weak and naked."

Twenty-five years later, in 1966, one of the survivors from the Repulse, Petty Officer Norman Edwards, dived into the blue, barracuda and shark-filled waters in a poignant ceremony held by the British Navy to mark the sinking of the ship. The aim was to attach a flag to the Repulse.

Edwards said, "I volunteered to dive. The sight of that flag flying in the water as though it was fluttering in the wind brought a lump to my throat. Memories of the ship and the men I had known aboard her came flooding back.

"Repulse was lying on the bottom like a huge cathedral."

Japanese soldiers preparing to cross a river in Malaya

I was very frightened that the British would discover our numerical weakness and lack of supplies.

— Lieutenant-General Tomoyuki Yamashita, head of the Japanese 25th Army, which conquered Singapore.

I suppose you will shove the little men off!

— Governor of Singapore, Sir Shenton Thomas to Lieutenant-General Arthur Percival, Army Commander of Malaya, when told of the Japanese forces landing in North Malaya on December 8, 1942.

Japanese soldiers crossing the Singora River

The Invasion

"We had beaten the 'Invincible Fortress' drum so loudly that we had fooled ourselves, not the enemy."
— *Brigadier Ivan Simson, Chief Engineer, Malaya.*

At 4.15 am on December 8, 1941, pilot Katsusaku Takahashi flew in low over Tengah Airbase as he hunted his target. Having flown 700 miles from Saigon, he carefully picked out his quarry and launched a bomb that fell with a whining, eerie scream, signalling the start of the battle for Fortress Singapore.

With him was Lieutenant Haruki Iki, the leader of the famous Kanoya Air Corps who later sank the British battleships, the Prince of Wales and Repulse. Iki recalled, "We also bombed an oil tank at Seletar Air Base and for days after that, the fire just went on and on. That was two months before the February invasion. But as I watched the smoke rise from the fire, I had the feeling that Singapore would fall in a very short time."

Singapore was brightly lit that fateful December morning. Apart from the top echelons of the defence forces, few people on the island knew that the Japanese had landed on the north coast of Malaya just a few hours earlier.

When Sir Shenton Thomas, the Governor and nominal Commander-in-Chief of the military forces, was awoken by a phone call from the Army Commander of Malaya, Lieutenant-General Arthur Percival, at 1.15 am and informed that Japanese troops had landed in Kota Baru, he said, "I suppose you will shove the little men off."

Sir Shenton was not totally enamoured of the wiry, tall Percival, a brilliant staff officer who unfortunately was quite untried as a commander.

For his part, the Governor did not think it necessary to alert the Air Raid Precautions office. Instead, he ordered the local police to round up all the Japanese males on the island before he and his wife went out to the balcony and sipped coffee while looking over the brightly lit island.

Truly Sir Shenton had little inkling of the calibre of the enemy he was facing, especially the charismatic Lieutenant-General Tomoyuki Yamashita who was to lead the forces of the Japanese Twenty-Fifth Army, consisting of about 60,000 troops right to his doorstep in just over two months.

Three hours later, the phone rang again. Japanese planes had been spotted heading towards Singapore. They were barely twenty-five miles away. Minutes later, the first bombs fell.

The main targets of the seventeen Japanese planes were the Seletar and Tengah airbases, which boasted Hurricanes, fighter planes fitted with machine guns for downing enemy bombers. "We never bombed the city, just the air bases. We attacked not because we wished to, but because we had to fight the British," Iki maintained.

But Singaporeans tell a different story:

In the pre-dawn darkness of Chinatown's Trengganu Street, people were preparing for another day of work when the first bombs fell. Agnes Leong, an occupant of Chinatown, described the scene: "In the top floor of a crumbling three-storey shophouse, mother had just finished preparing the feeding bottle for yet another round of baby brother Jimmy's ceaseless nocturnal feedings.

"There was no warning and no ARP's shouts when the low, ominous wail that was to become so terrifyingly familiar in the next few months burst into a thunderous crash that sent her sprawling onto a table. Staggering up, she gaped at the empty space where a wall should have been. The carnage in her room was complete. Lusty, wailing Jimmy was now a bloody pulp on the bed.

"She stared at the feeding bottle, still intact, as though preserved by an Almighty with an abounding sense of humour, and slowly toppled into merciful darkness."

Among other casualties of that first bombing raid was a young man, Corporal Raymond Lee of the Chinese Volunteer Force, who had been standing guard outside the Chartered Bank.

Dr Yap Pheng Geck, who headed the Chinese Volunteer Force, wrote, "When the first Japanese bombs rained down on Singapore, I was in Raffles Square with my Sergeant-Major, Lee Kian Wah, in the course of my rounds of inspection of defence posts under my command. I immediately rushed back to my station in the basement of Ocean Building and telephoned Headquarters, telling them, 'A bomb just dropped here.'

"But I was told I was talking nonsense.

"I asked, 'Didn't you hear it?'

"They said, 'Yes, yes, yes, but it may be a firing practice somewhere.'

"That was the reaction at Headquarters."

Such confusion reigned throughout the ranks.

Private Joginder Singh of the 4th Battalion Straits Settlements Volunteer Forces was awoken by "the wailing of sirens, the sound of anti-aircraft shells bursting and distant bomb explosions. I jumped out of my camp bed in St Patrick's School where I was stationed and joined my comrades outside, all looking at the small, silvery planes in arrowhead formation caught in the beams of searchlights. Someone was talking excitedly, saying that these were Japanese planes bombing the naval base; others said it could not be, the Japanese were so far away.

"A private shouted from his camp bed to us, 'Come back, all of you, it's only an air raid practice. Go back to sleep.' "

Over at the Raffles Hotel, the staff rushed in a feverish panic into the hotel's garage, which served as a bomb shelter. Some even ran into the cold room where the meats were kept. Shivering from the fear and the cold, they stared vacantly at each other, waiting for the shelling to stop.

When the thunderous rumble of bombers faded

and the floor shook only from the air conditioning, someone said, "It's over!"

Cautiously, one of the staff opened the door and peered out. The others followed tentatively.

Poo Shean Han, then a thirty-year-old cook, left immediately for home. There was no public transport, but opposite the Odeon Cinema, there were lorries picking up corpses. Poo stopped in his tracks at the sight. He did not return to work that day.

Chin Kee Onn, author of three books on Malaya, wrote of the disbelief with which the news was received.

"Over breakfast, the morning music from the radio was suddenly interrupted and we heard the announcement that Singapore had been bombed by Japanese planes in the early hours before daybreak.

"The news, of course, was startling. I had always thought that Japan would never dare start a war in the East by attacking Malaya as she would then be forced to take on Britain and America. And if Japan could not even conquer China, which was then militarily weak, how could she take on the combined might of the two powers?

"I had been so completely overcome by the power of British propaganda as were hundreds of thousands of others in Malaya."

L. A. Duckworth, another Singapore resident, remembered surveying the damage the following morning. "My wife and I drove into town to see what damage had been done. In Raffles Place we saw that Robinson's had taken a whack. We were prevented from entering Market

Street by the police, but were informed that several of the Chettiar business houses had been demolished by direct hits, with some loss of life.

"Driving back over Anderson Bridge we noticed that the Victoria Theatre had sustained some damage, especially the clock tower, although the clock itself was still functioning.

"A couple of days later, Singaporeans were amused by a large notice on the verandah of the Memorial Hall, that read, 'THEY CAN'T STOP OUR CLOCK!'

"But the boast was rather short-lived, for on subsequent air raids the Japanese deliberately machine-gunned that clock, silencing it for the duration of the war."

The media, however, downplayed that first attack. In fact, the Malaya Tribune newspaper dismissed the Japanese landing at Kota Baru where 700 soldiers were killed or wounded and another 1,200 drowned or missing with a report headlined, "Malaya Hits Back!" A second caption underneath the first read, "Japanese retreat after Kelantan landing."

The Tribune's report on the bombing of Singapore began with the headline, "Singapore takes it — with a grin."

It said, "Singapore's civilian population received its baptism of fire last night with gallantry and brave acceptance," and added in an editorial, "The fact that the first air raid on Singapore lasted only a few minutes is proof of our preparedness."

It failed to mention that the Japanese did not lose a

single plane in that attack. Air-Vice Marshal C. W. Pulford was to later admit that the British planes were not allowed to take off to challenge the invaders because the anti-aircraft gunners were considered so incompetent that the military chiefs were worried they would shoot down their own planes.

The poor state of preparation was compounded by a number of problems. There was a misjudgement of the severity of the threat the Japanese posed. For instance, critical information about the capabilities of the deadly Japanese Zero aeroplane was lost in a morass of paperwork and was never communicated to the proper authorities, leaving the island dependent on the untested Brewster Buffalo aircraft, which were to perform poorly against the Japanese aircraft.

The air, naval and infantry forces were also caught in a bickering and hostile rivalry that led them to adopt defence plans that were uncoordinated. In 1936, the Air Force built airstrips in the north of Malaya in places so inaccessible that the Army refused to man them.

The lack of cooperation was exacerbated by bungled senior appointments. Finally, in May 1941, Brigadier Ivan Simson was sent to Singapore as Chief Engineer of Malaya — the best appointment yet, but with his hands tied without sufficient authorisation from the War Office to remedy the fundamental weaknesses he discovered in the island's defence. The brigadier found an endemic shortage of arms and trained personnel as well as a misplaced emphasis on a southern coastal defence that simply could not be remedied in time. To Simson, the fate of Singapore soon became apparent — it was doomed.

Yet the Tribune reporter gave an upbeat account of the scene after the bombing. He avoided any mention of which areas were hit. But word had already got around that the bombs had hit Raffles Place, Empress Place, Market Street and Chinatown, where most of Singapore's population was concentrated.

The Tribune report merely said, "At the worst bombed streets, Chinese whose homes were blasted were busy retrieving personal possessions while cracking jokes with sympathetic onlookers. One chap, whose head was bound and covered in dust and blood was cheerful while waiting for his *makan* from the Air Raid Post canteen."

The careful reader might have noticed that The Straits Times did give an indication of the casualties when it reported a brief meeting of the Legislative Council with Sir Shenton, where the Governor mentioned sixty dead and 133 wounded. That report was buried in the back page.

But news of the casualties spread like wildfire in the crammed quarters of Chinatown. Their confidence shaken, the Chinese provision shopkeepers immediately abandoned their credit system. Not accustomed to carrying cash around, the *Tuan Besar* or "Big Sir" as the Europeans were called, suddenly found they could not buy the basics with the stroke of a pen.

Othman Wok, later to become Social Affairs Minister and at that time a student heading for his first Cambridge exam paper on the morning the bombs fell, said, "The whole of Singapore city was on the move. Lorries were loaded and people moved this way and that, without any sense of purpose. You could feel the tension in the air."

The British immediately moved to garner the support of communal leaders to help organise a local resistance force. The Governor lifted the ban on the communists and several other Chinese associations. He also appointed Tan Kah Kee, a prominent leader of the Chinese community, as the head of the Overseas Chinese Mobilisation Council.

Thus was born Dalforce, the vaunted Chinese armed resistance that was put together hastily by the Special Branch of the Malayan Police from the recruits drawn by Tan Kah Kee's council.

Meanwhile, the highly motivated Japanese army drove the Allied forces, mainly British and Indian troops, down the west coast of Malaya over an amazing sixty-eight days. The Allies were not prepared for the guerilla warfare tactics of the advancing enemy.

The Japanese overran Alor Star on December 12. Four days later, they took Penang. They were soon in Ipoh and by January 11, they had walked into the Malayan capital of Kuala Lumpur, the rubber centre of the world and an important communications centre.

By the end of January, the Japanese were chasing the Allies across the Causeway. The last of 30,000 Allied troops retreated across the Causeway at 8 am. The Japanese harried the retreating forces with low flying aircraft, but held back their air attack against the totally vulnerable retreating troops because they did not want to cause more damage to the Causeway.

With the retreat of the Allies to Singapore, the Japanese were now in total control of the Peninsula. Their morale was at its highest point as their objective now lay almost within reach. They promptly cut off the water supply from Gunong Pulai in Johor state to Singapore, causing a critical water shortage on the island. Singapore now had to rely on the limited water supply from its storage reservoirs, which could only last a few more days.

Then the Japanese forces toned down their attack as they regrouped and prepared for the final assault.

The writing was on the wall. Fortress Singapore looked painfully vulnerable.

Singapore went under curfew from January 29. No one was to be on the streets between 9 pm and 5 am, but this did not stop those who were determined to escape from the island. Among them was Tan Kah Kee, who knew he would be high on the wanted list of the Japanese forces because he was the rallying point of overseas Chinese opposition to the Japanese invasion of China and subsequently Southeast Asia. His nephew, Tan Keong Choon, recalled, "When my uncle and his friends heard that the British were requisitioning all marine transport, they fled to Sumatra on a motor launch. He did not even have time to say goodbye to the family."

Yamashita moved into the Johor Sultan's palace,

the Istana Hijau, from where he had a commanding view of Singapore. The palace, which dominated the skyline, was a clear target for the British planes and a risky proposition for an army headquarters. Nonetheless, it offered obvious advantages as an observation post and communications centre.

Wrote Colonel Masanobu Tsuji, the mastermind of the attack on Singapore, "From the palace, the naval port of Seletar lay beneath one's eyes, and Tengah aerodrome appeared as if it could be grasped in the hand.

"It was within easy range of the enemy artillery, and at times machine-gun bullets came flying past, for the enemy lines were not more than two kilometres distant."

For their part, the Allies simply had no clue that Yamashita had stationed himself in the palace. Thus, they never seriously considered bombing it.

The two forces squared off across the narrow strip of water, one marshalling all its strength to attack, the other struggling to shape up a good defence.

On February 1, there were about one million civilians on the island, including refugees from Malaya. The Allied troops numbered about 100,000, outnumbering the Japanese by two to one. However, as an army on the run, forced to make a last-ditch stand, their morale was shattered. There was a great "ballyhoo" among some of the soldiers, wrote the Governor, who directed his military chiefs to put a stop to it at once, saying, "We cannot allow our own men to riot, and refuse it to the Asiatics."

One of the last contingents to arrive was the British

18th Division. They had stepped off their troop ships only two days before the retreat across the Causeway. They were unaccustomed to the tropical heat and not physically fit enough for active service. But there was little choice. In a few days they were to fight for their lives.

The Allies were led by six officers: Lt-General Percival, Army Commander of Malaya;

Lt-General Sir Lewis Heath, the head of the 3rd Army Corps, the 9th and 11th British-Indian Divisions, which were greatly reduced in strength by heavy casualties and losses in Malaya;

Lt-General Gordon Bennett, head of the Australian forces commanding two brigades of the 8th Australian Division and the 2/4th Machine gun Battalion, also depleted by fighting on the mainland;

Major-General B. W. Key; Major-General Keith Simmons, the Fortress Commander; and the newly arrived Major-General Beckwith-Smith of the 18th Division.

In addition, there were also three British Army Indian Brigades — the 28th, the 44th and the 45th; and two brigades of the Volunteer Army, made up of Chinese and Malay recruits.

On the Japanese side, there was only the 25th Army led by Lt-General Yamashita, consisting of three divisions: the Imperial Guards Division led by Lt-General Nishimura, the 5th Division led by Lt-Gen Matsui and the 18th Division led by Lt-General Mutaguchi. They also had the support of the 3rd Tank Brigade.

Percival had a choice of two alternative strategies

to defend Singapore. He could either spread the bulk of his forces thinly across the northern coastline facing Johor, or he could hold back the bulk of the forces ready to counterattack the Japanese wherever they chose to land.

He chose the former. He was confident that the Japanese would try to land on the area east of the Causeway where the Naval Base and two airfields were located. So he moved the 11th and the newly arrived 18th divisions to the east from Changi to the Causeway, which he called the Northern Area.

The Western Area, from the Jurong River to the Causeway was given to the Australian Division to defend together with one Indian Infantry Brigade.

Finally, the rest of the island was designated the Southern Area, to be held by the rest of the forces.

Percival had spread the forces thin across the island, with no hope of quick reinforcements for any one force that might be under severe attack. He also miscalculated by thinking the Japanese would attack on the northeastern coast. They set up a decoy action on that front, but sent their main force in by the northwest. It was left to the Australians and the Indians to stop them.

As the Japanese prepared for the final assault on Singapore, one thing that worried them was the possibility that when they attempted to cross the Straits, the British would simply flood it with their six months supply of fuel from the Naval Base and set it on fire. This scenario was raised with Yamashita earlier by a German general. So the Japanese tested the theory by setting a small pond on fire in Johor. The coat of oil on the still water blazed fiercely, but the Japanese assessed that the tides of the Johor Straits would inhibit such an effect.

In any case, to play it safe they blasted the oil reserves on February 3 and 4 with heavy artillery fire. The burning oil covered the whole of Singapore in thick, black, choking fumes.

Tension was high among the Japanese High Command on the night of February 8 as Japanese troops prepared to cross into Singapore.

When the second-hand struck eleven o'clock, their forces exploded into action. Thousands of rounds of ammunition rained on the western shore where battle-weary Australian and Indian soldiers were holed up. The deadly fire from across the Causeway snapped the Allies' wire communication lines, shot out their searchlights, blew up pillboxes and pinned the Allied troops in their trenches.

Under the covering fire, the crack troops of the Japanese 5th and 18th battalions slipped into the Johor Straits on their motorised launches and sped across the water. The first wave did not meet strong resistance from the Australians and Indians, who had to guess where the advancing troops were. The defenders shot blindly at the water level, hoping to hit the advancing troops.

Japanese mastermind Tsuji described the fate of one troop leader in a characteristically heroic way, "Lance-Corporal Yamamoto, standing at the bow of a raft made of three launches lashed together, was continually drenched with spray thrown up by enemy shells hitting the water around the boats. While fully loaded with men of the second line of assault troops, a shell burst on the gunwale of one of the launches composing the raft, killing the other two coxswains and severely damaging their boats.

"Yamamoto was the only man left capable of handling the launches, which had fifty men aboard. He landed them on the enemy shore and then collapsed like a falling tree.

"When the squad commander of the troops lifted him in his arms he saw his lungs portruding through his ribs. Yamamoto had said nothing about his wound until he landed the troops in his charge and while the squad commander still held him in his arms, he said, 'Long live the Emperor! I am indebted to you for your kind assistance. Excuse me for going a step ahead of you.'

"And so saying, he breathed his last."

The Allies were less eloquent about their heroics, which were certainly present. Even in the midst of the barrage from across the Causeway, an Allied gunboat tried valiantly to "interfere with the passage of our troops across the Straits", as Tsuji put it. An artillery shell sank the gunboat.

The advancing Japanese troops waded through hip-deep mud in the face of enemy gunfire to secure the waterfront. Shortly after midnight, a blue flare shot up on the 5th Division front, followed shortly by another flare from the 18th Division — they had landed as planned.

In the Istana Hijau, Yamashita and the other officers were speechless with emotion. "The moonlight shone dimly on tears flowing down all our cheeks," wrote Tsuji.

In the early morning hours of February 9, the Japanese forces flooded across the island, heading straight for Tengah Airbase. They focused their attack on Pasir Laba and Kranji Creek in the northwest to cut off the Allies while they pushed towards Tengah Airfield.

By dawn, more than 5,000 Japanese soldiers had secured three miles of coast. They continued to overwhelm the Allies with their sheer numbers and determined sallies. Two Australian battalions suffered heavy casualties, losing four company commanders. To save the rest from being cut off in their positions, the Australians were pulled back.

A "really Homeric fight" was put up by 600 clerks and drivers near the Tengah airbase under Major A. E. Saggers of the West Australian machine gun battalion. Armed only with rifles, they fought together with the Indian garrison to hold their positions against the Japanese 5th division.

But the Japanese took control of Tengah Airbase by the night of February 9, less than forty-eight hours after they had launched their first land attack. They found soup and fresh bread still lying in the mess hall, and suitcases of clothes strewn about.

The Australians were reduced to pockets of resistance. Over the next forty-eight hours, the surviving members regrouped with the main Australian line, now pushed back to between Sungei Kranji and Sungei Jurong.

The Japanese continued their spirited attack and

pushed the Allies' defence line to the main road between the villages of Bukit Panjang and Bukit Timah. Although there was fierce fighting in some areas, it was clear that on the whole the Allies' defence was steadily unravelling. Australian soliders who had been heavily shelled were found wandering on the roads.

Army Major Hotsaku Shimada led 100 tanks onto the island. He said, "On February 9, 1942, we advanced on the northern side of Singapore. For six days, we fought hard as we moved southwards. I came through to Bukit Timah, to the race course, and finally reached a cemetery near the MacRitchie Reservoir, where we attacked the British."

Some of the fiercest fighting of the region was to occur here as the Japanese decided to take the Bukit Timah fortress before the Allies had any chance to regroup and counterattack. The Japanese commanders decided not to wait for artillery and instead relied on the cloak of night to assault the British positions on February 10.

Yamashita orchestrated the attack from a command post on the edge of the jungle on the southern part of Tengah Airbase. The 5th Division attacked from the north side of the Choa Chu Kang Road. The 18th Division advanced by the south side of the road.

The attack was successful. Bukit Timah Hill fell into Japanese hands before dawn. They now had a stranglehold on Singapore's water supply, which they promptly cut off.

Once news spread that the Japanese had landed in

Singapore, the city centre was a mass of petrified civilians fleeing in all directions. They mingled with equally bewildered Australian and Indian stragglers.

Families split and went in different directions of the island to ensure that at least some of them survived. The luckier ones had contacts in the villages where they stayed in attap huts or even in chicken coops.

The evacuation was followed by looting. In Singapore, it was so prevalent, particularly in the local sectors of the city where the public markets stood, that the stalls looked as though they had been descended on by a swarm of locusts. Almost all survivors of the war remember scenes of looting or participating in them. Civilian Chan Kwee Sung, then a teenager, remembered how he succumbed to the mob mentality, scaled a wall and risked his life for several Nafi beer mugs.

Lee Tian Soo, then a teenager of seventeen, recounted his own escapade, "I saw smoke coming from the godowns near the present Riverside Hotel. I went to investigate and found that the British were burning the goods there because they didn't want them to fall into Japanese hands. I thought, why not get some things for my family?

"Some of the looters smashed the doors of the Bank of China godown with lorries. I managed to get a hold of some bales of cloth. As I made my way home, barely being able to see over the bundle of bales, some Indian soldiers, who were much bigger than me, snatched some of the loot away."

"I was very disappointed with what I managed to

bring home after I saw some of the things others had managed to rip off, like big, big cases of provisions."

Lee also remembered the thrill as a gawky teenager of smelling the vapour of expensive liquor in the air that volunteers laboured to destroy because they were afraid that the conquering Japanese soldiers would later get drunk on it and become more brutal. He recalled, "Their job was to break the bottles in the huge drain beside Customs House and let it drain into the sea. When we cycled past the drain, we could smell brandy and whisky!"

The banks were determined that their British currency should not fall into the hands of the Japanese. Trusted officials fed a staggering $5 million into a furnace. Businesses and individuals were also encouraged to destroy their cash, with compensation to be made at the end of the war.

On Wednesday, February 10, the Japanese artillery pounded Singapore continuously. The Governor witnessed the sight of the Commander-in-Chief of the Southeast Asian forces, Lieutenant-General Archibald Wavell, "thumping his hands on his knees and saying, 'It shouldn't have happened' over and over again." Wavell escaped from the island that night.

The next day, Thursday, February 11, Yamashita sent a message to Percival, urging him to surrender. The note, which was dropped in the British sector by aeroplane, read:

The Japanese Commander to the British Com-

mander:

In a spirit of chivalry we have the honour of advising your surrender. Your army, founded on the traditional spirit of Great Britain, is defending Singapore, which is completely isolated, and raising the fame of Great Britain by the utmost exertions and heroic fighting. I disclose my respects from my inmost feelings.

Nevertheless the war situation is already determined, and in the meantime the surrender of Singapore is imminent. From now on resistance is futile and merely increases the danger to the million civilian inhabitants without good reason, exposing them to infliction of pain by fire and sword.

Furthermore, we do not feel you will increase the fame of the British Army by further resistance. From first to last, our counsel is that Your Excellency will cease to think of meaningless resistance and from now on, yielding to our advice, promptly and immediately suspend the action extending over the whole British battlefront.

It is expected that you will take measures to dispatch an army messenger as stated below. If, on the contrary, you continue resistance as previously, it will be difficult to bear with patience from a humanitarian point of view and inevitably we must continue an intense attack against Singapore. Ending this advice we show respect towards Your Excellency.

1. The army messenger's route of advance shall be by Bukit Timah Road.

2. The army messenger, hoisting a white flag as

*well as the British flag, will be escorted by a number of
soldiers as protection.*

It was signed by Yamashita.

However, Percival continued receiving instructions
from his superiors to resist the Japanese invasion. He also
believed that Singapore could somehow hold out until
help arrived.

His fellow officers did not share his confidence,
and they had good reasons. Everywhere, there was destruction. The sixty-million pound floating dock had been
sunk, ships were burning in the harbour, the flames licking
the water, vehicles of every description were burning down
to a shapeless mass. As people wandered out slowly into
the streets, they ducked at the sound of the odd explosion
as oil drums exploded here and there. The island had an
atmosphere of oily smoke, dust and soot.

Dr Cecily Williams of the Tan Tock Seng Hospital
wrote, "When I drove about, the town was full of evacuating and deserting soldiers, most of them Australians
looking utterly disorganised and defeated. They had thrown
off their equipment, they were looting the shops or sitting
in rows with their boots off down near the quays; they
were pushing women and children out of the way to get to
the buildings when bombs were falling nearby; they were
crowding females and children off the boats that were
getting away. It was a terrible show."

On Friday, February 12, Bennett, leader of the
Australian forces, marshalled all available Australian troops

to make a final stand at Reformatory Road. Even non-combatant troops were brought in to fortify the perimeter. They were joined by the British 18th Division as it fell back against the blitzkrieg of the Japanese forces.

Five thousand Australians and Britishers held the line with hardly any air cover against the Japanese land and air onslaught. General Bennett wrote in his diary, "I consider the end is near."

On Saturday, February 13, the Japanese engineers finished repairs to the damaged Causeway and the rest of their tanks rumbled onto the streets of Singapore. Yamashita, who had not received any reply to his surrender offer, conveyed his wrath at being ignored with the most savage bombardment of the city yet. Shells pounded the island at intervals of barely two seconds for hours on end, sounding like amplified machine-gun fire. Fires raged everywhere but the precious water needed to put them out was now barely trickling into the city.

It was during this period that the brutal massacre of nearly 400 people in the Alexandra Hospital occurred. A British Army surgeon, Sidney Nardell, witnessed the massacre. He said, "The hospital, filled with wounded, was plainly marked everywhere with large red crosses. It lay in no man's land between the advancing Japanese troops and our own troops."

The Japanese troops claimed there were Indian troops within the hospital who had fired on them. On that pretext, "they entered the building firing their rifles and machine guns, and throwing hand grenades indiscriminately. Within a few minutes ten medical officers were killed. The Japanese entered the operating theatre where Captain Tom Smiley was trying to operate."

Nardell said nearly all the operating theatre staff were bayonetted on the spot or shot. Even the patient on the table was bayonetted.

"About 350 Royal Army Medical Corps personnel, walking wounded and others were marched out of the hospital and bayonetted."

The surgeon himself escaped by pretending to be one of the dead. He was eventually caught, and spent the next three-and-a-half years in the prison camps.

Another chilling encounter of being caught in no man's land came from Chan Kwee Sung.

"It was a Sunday, the eve of the Lunar New Year, but there was no reunion dinner because my father and I were separated from the rest of the family who had taken refuge further away at Tai Seng village. My father and I stayed put at a shophouse at Paya Lebar Road where he was a shop assistant.

"It was unnaturally quiet. All shops and houses were closed and the main road was deserted, in contrast to the past few days when it was cluttered with military vehicles. Only a slow moving line of widely spaced puggareed Doggras with rifles and bayonets ready, plodded along on each side of the road heading towards Serangoon."

"We prepared whatever dinner we could in the ominous calm that prevailed and I was halfway through my chicken drumstick when the fighting started. There was a terrific bang that sent us running for cover under a double bed with a thick mattress on top for such a contingency.

"It marked the beginning of a street battle and it seemed as if all hell had broken loose. There was the incessant chatter of machine guns, the intermittent barking of rifles punctuated by frenzied yells and screams of the warring parties. In our smoke-enshrouded haven, we could hear bullets hit walls and other objects above us. The sounds were unforgettable and if not for their gruesome results, the crackling of gunfire would have done magnificent justice in ushering in the New Year of the Horse.

"We sat out the battle that lasted till morning. On stepping out, we saw a Japanese flag flying from a house that must have been used as a command post."

Nonetheless on the same day, Monday, February 15 — the day Singapore was to surrender — The Straits Times came out with a front page that defiantly announced, "Singapore shall stand!"

In actual fact, food and ammunition was low, and most importantly, the reservoirs were in enemy hands and even the hospitals were without water for the past twenty-four hours.

Early that Monday morning, the hopelessness of the situation finally sank in on Wavell who sent Percival a message, saying, "So long as you are in a position to inflict losses and damage to the enemy and your troops are physically capable of doing so, you must fight on," but added significantly, "When you are fully satisfied that is no longer possible, I give you discretion to cease resistance."

That was all the confirmation the military chiefs needed. When Percival called a conference of senior officers to assess the situation, they unanimously agreed that there was nothing to be served by further resistance. They decided to surrender.

Rumours of the surrender spread like wildfire through the island as rumours always do, hours before the actual surrender. But as it was just one more rumour in a barrage of rumours that had circulated since the hostilities began, the Allied forces continued to do battle in many areas.

Major Hotsaku Shimada said, "I remember especially the two hours before the British surrender. The British army blew up one of our tanks and one of my men was killed in the tank. We were still attacking the British military in the early morning when we saw the white flag that came out from behind the cemetery."

The Governor simply refused to meet the Japanese, so his acting Colonial Secretary, Hugh Fraser, was sent in his place to negotiate the surrender with Yamashita. Fraser took with him Major Wylde and Brigadier Newbiggin.

The trio made the hazardous journey with difficulty, finally reaching a Japanese post at Bukit Timah. Carrying only a limp, white flag, they warily approached the soldiers.

To their amazement, when the Japanese soldiers finally grasped the aim of their mission, they whipped out their cameras and began a prolonged photo session. Smiling and exultant at being the first on the spot at this momentous event, they took turns to capture the historic moment with the Britishers. They tried different angles and continued like that until there was no more film left.

Only then did they send word to their general about the British delegation. Eventually Colonel Sugita, who was in charge of Intelligence and had drafted the surrender offer from Yamashita, materialised with a letter from the Tiger of Malaya. Sugita, who was in a plaster cast because of a broken collar bone, listened impassively as Newbiggin tried to explain what his superior officer back at Fort Canning had in mind.

Sugita then spoke, explaining that Yamashita would stand for nothing less than an unconditional surrender from Percival himself at 4.30 that afternoon. The colonel also demanded that the Allied forces lay down their arms immediately and remain in their positions. As a first indication of their capitulation, they were to fly a Japanese flag atop the highest building in the land at the time, the Cathay Building. Having made himself clear, Sugita handed Newbiggin a huge Japanese flag.

When Fraser returned to Fort Canning at about four o'clock he handed Percival the statement of demands in which Yamashita scoffed at any suggestion of negotiations. He wanted only an outright surrender of the island and would not order a ceasefire until Percival ceded Singapore to him. He also said he would deal with only Percival himself.

For his part, Yamashita guaranteed the British delegation safe passage and even promised to have a car waiting for them near the minefield at Adam Road to take them to Ford Motors.

The surrender of the "impregnable citadel" took place in the Ford Motor Company's head office at Bukit Timah Road. It was a pale and dispirited Percival who walked into the boardroom of Ford Motor Company with his three staff officers that evening. The Tiger of Malaya was in a belligerent mood, mainly because he was not certain of Percival's true intentions and felt his own position to be weak.

For Yamashita knew something that the Allies did not. The Japanese forces were heavily outnumbered and low on ammunition from the heavy bombardment of Singapore. Yamashita also harboured the added fear that Percival was perhaps stalling, so that reinforcements could be rushed in. The Tiger of Malaya said, "I was very frightened all the time that the British would discover our numerical weakness and lack of supplies and force me into disastrous street fighting."

He refused to negotiate or enter into discussions. Instead he stubbornly insisted that Percival sign the surrender document on the dotted line. At one point, Yamashita shot up from his chair and blustered before a visibly cowed Percival.

After Percival gave in, the Japanese senior officers returned to their Army Headquarters where they were greeted with a celebratory spread of dried cuttlefish, chestnuts and wine, gifts from the Emperor. Yamashita told his staff, "Thank you very much. From now on, you may drink sake whenever you like."

The Japanese lost 1,700 men in the final week-long battle for Singapore, with another 3,400 injured. But they had captured about 100,000 prisoners of war.

On the island, the deafening roar of the war was replaced by the sound of crackling fires that still raged that night. The huge Japanese flag flapped menacingly from the Cathay Building.

In just over two months after the first air raid, the Impregnable Fortress was now in Japanese hands.

The Occupation

"In those days, when someone left home, there was every chance that he would never return."
— *Mr Lee Tian Soo, a civilian who was in his late teens during the Occupation.*

When the Japanese tanks rolled in on February 15, there were cries of *"Banzai!"* from some who lined the streets to watch. "Japanese flags just sprung up from nowhere on people's doors. I presume there were commercially-minded chaps who exploited the situation," said George Bogaars who later became the head of Independent Singapore's civil service.

Eze Nathan, a prominent member of the local Jewish community, took in the scene from the balcony of his family home in Amber Mansions as the victors marched into the city.

"What we saw was a ragged procession of worn-out, unkempt figures scarcely recognisable as soldiers, let alone victors, more indeed in keeping with the stories circulating before the Japanese victories in North Malaya! These were the opponents, the supermen, who had forced us to capitulate," he wrote.

"At the rear were two tanks with heavy guns and

69

seven smaller tanks. We were to become very familiar with this armoury. As the tanks made their appearance, disappearance and reappearance in the first days of the Occupation, I was reminded of a school production of Julius Caesar where the same few schoolboys, masquerading as a full army, marched boldly onstage, then off, dashing around behind the flimsy back-cloth to reappear from behind the other wings."

What Nathan saw was not the main force of the Japanese army. They were, in fact, mainly the leading force of military police sent to establish control over the island. As the Japanese took up their positions all over Singapore, apart from their few supporters shouting "*Banzai!*", they found the streets mainly deserted as the local population wisely stayed indoors. Stores were closed as shopkeepers joined the self-imposed curfew.

However, on Orchard Road, the famous Cold Storage was still open. In fact, it was extremely busy as the manager and his small staff of faithfuls served the Britishers and Australians as word spread quickly about this last-chance shopping opportunity. Many of the customers were after items such as razor blades because they expected to be imprisoned by the Japanese.

Among the first orders the Japanese gave was for all European troops to assemble and march with their gear to Selarang Barracks in the Changi area. George Aspinall, who hid a camera in his gear and made a photographic record of the Occupation, described the scene: "If you had an aerial view, you would have seen a long line of European troops marching towards Changi from various parts of the island over the next three days. Those who couldn't walk were taken by ambulances that were still in operation.

"I will never forget that march. The local people were all lined-up beside the road watching us walk past. The Chinese were particularly sympathetic, offering us bananas, coconuts and drinks of water when they could. I think they were as bewildered as we were that we had suddenly become prisoners of war."

The European prisoners of war spent the next three-and-a-half years in detention. Among the prisoners were Sir Shenton and his wife, Percival and his senior officers such as Ivan Simson. Bennett escaped to Australia shortly before the fall of Singapore, where he faced considerable controversy for having arrived home safely while his troops were incarcerated on the island. Sir Shenton, Percival and Simson, among others, were moved to Taiwan in August where they spent the rest of their prison days.

In the first twenty-four hours, a quick order also went out to clear the beds in the local hospitals to make way for the Japanese war wounded. Nathan was one of the locals detained to help clear the hospitals. "I was asked to go with some Rover Scouts and a party of Medical Auxiliary Service to the Alexander Military Hospital in Pasir Panjang to help 'clean the wards'.

"What we found defied description. The Japanese had perpetrated a monstrous crime — the mindless bayonetting of patients, nurses and doctors. It was our task to

71

help collect and place the bodies in military trucks for burial. We were sent on the same mission to many other places. Malacca Street and Raffles Place were scenes of exceptional carnage.

"After these experiences, evacuating the General Hospital was slightly less harrowing. We had twenty-four hours to evacuate a thousand patients, some seriously ill. Our instructions were to leave behind the drugs and medical equipment for the wounded Japanese, but doctors and nurses managed to smuggle out a small quantity."

He added, "Many owed their lives in the next few months, to their foresight and courage. Convoys of ambulances took civilian patients to the Miyako Hospital, while the mental patients were dispatched to an island nearby."

Patients were also sent to the Cricket Club, the Singapore Club and the Victoria Hall. Children were sent to Woodbridge Hospital and babies were simply given away to anyone who would have them.

The next day, February 16, a Monday, the Nipponese Army High Command issued an order directed at the European civilians:

Citizens of all nations at war with Japan, including members of the Chungking Government, are to proceed to the Padang at 10.30 am on Tuesday, 17th February 1942, with enough clothing for ten days, but they must carry the packages themselves. Sick and wounded civilians are to remain in their homes or in the hospital. Their addresses are to be recorded.

"Internees will be accommodated in two camps, one for the men and one for women. No servants are permitted, except of the same race. Those engaged in public services are to carry on and wear arm bands signifying 'Service'.

"It is unnecessary to bring food."

The order drew 1,197 men, 145 women and thirty-seven children, a few of them in their cars. They went to the Padang with absolutely no idea of what was going to happen. As they had been ordered to carry their own bags, most people took only carry bags and small suitcases with their valuables, toiletries and some change of clothing.

The Japanese herded the men to one side of the Padang, and the women and children to the other. The children soon began crying under the hot sun, but there was nothing their parents could do as they anxiously awaited orders from the Japanese on their fate.

The Japanese officers themselves seemed uncertain as to what to do with them. Meanwhile, in the shade under the trees by the road, the Asian spectators turned up to watch the British Empire crumble, not without sympathy.

Lunch time came and went. Some who had brought food shared it with others who had taken the Japanese order at face value. But those who suspected that their fates would not be decided quickly, did not share their meals with anyone.

Finally, at two in the afternoon, a severe-looking officer stepped up to the group and shouted something in Japanese. It soon became apparent that the Japanese wanted them to march. The old, infirm and children were allowed to board the cars. Where space permitted, the vehicles were allowed to accommodate the heavier bags, like suitcases, but the remaining luggage had to be carried personally.

It was a very slow, long march for these privileged people who had never walked any distance on the island out of necessity. The men were marched to Joo Chiat Police Station and the Karical Flats. The women were taken to two mansions near the old Roxy Cinema, where over the next two weeks other European women and children joined them, swelling their numbers to 400.

The Europeans remained in these temporary camps until the first two weeks of March when first the men and then the women and children were moved to Changi Prison where they spent the next three-and-a-half years.

Meanwhile, in another part of the city, on Tuesday morning, February 16, the day after the surrender, the Japanese were also rounding up the Asian soldiers. Among them was Private Joginder Singh, who marched towards the city through Bukit Timah Road with his volunteer unit, under Japanese guard. At several places along the road, the men had to hold their noses because of the stench of rotting corpses covered with swarms of flies.

The unit was led to Farrer Park, which was filling up with bewildered Indian, Malay and Chinese troops of

His Majesty's Government, dirty, unshaven and uncertain of their future under the Japanese.

There were soldiers pouring in from all sides of the field, but as Singh looked around, he noticed that there were very few Japanese guards. Realising that they could not possibly keep an eye on everyone, Singh sidled over to his commanding officer and outlined an escape plan. The officer said he could not take part in it himself, but nodded and wished Singh luck.

At an appropriate moment, cloaked by the confusion of hundreds more troops pouring in, Singh and six others slinked off to hide in the nearest building. They realised that they could not stay there for long, so they made a dash for the adjacent Kandang Kerbau Hospital, which at that time was known as the General Hospital.

Dozens of women were in various stages of labour in the hospital so the escapees could not hide in the wards. Singh and his compatriots hid under a staircase instead and stripped off their uniforms.

As they were undressing, a shadow loomed over them. They looked up to find a European nursing sister, speechless at the sight of the seven men stripping. But it did not take her long to get the picture. When she found her voice, she scolded them for deserting and threatened to report them to the police.

Singh and his mates did not wait to hear more. They scurried out of the hospital in their shorts and singlets and were soon mingling anonymously with the crowd in "Little India" nearby.

It is not clear how many others slipped out of Farrer Park that way, but the fate of those who remained was bleak. About 32,000 of them were Indians.

The Japanese knew the Indians' morale was low, and urged them to join the nationalist Indian National Army led by Subhas Chandra Bose, an anti-British Indian leader and ally of the Japanese. He led a militant Independence movement which scorned Mahatma Gandhi's non-violent Independence movement and believed that the only way India could shed the British yoke was to fight for its freedom.

It was a tempting offer. The Indians felt badly let down by the British, who had sent them, poorly equipped, to the worst battlefronts, in return for which all they could expect from a triumphant Britain was continued colonial rule. The Japanese, on the other hand, spoke of the defeated forces as Asian brothers and promised to help liberate India from British rule.

Nonetheless, more than half of the Indian prisoners refused to join the Japanese-sponsored Indian National Army (INA) in Singapore. Most of the professional soldiers refused the Japanese offer point-blank. These included the Gurkha forces, of whom not a single one could be persuaded to turn against the British.

Those who refused to side against the Japanese were tortured, and in many cases killed.

With the Indians at Farrer Park were 600 Malay soldiers. The Japanese urged them to renege their allegiance to the British and pledge support to their Emperor instead. There were eight Malay officers among the soldiers. When they repudiated the Japanese offer, they were summarily executed.

The Japanese told the remaining Malays that they would be sent home to the Peninsula. About 100 Malays climbed into trucks that the Japanese said would take them straight to the railway station. The rest were allowed to return to their families who were waiting for them in their temporary homes in Kampung Glam. As for the 100 who were taken away in the trucks, they were never seen again. It is believed that the *Kempeitai*, the dreaded Japanese military police, took them to an isolated spot where they were massacred. It is not clear how their bodies were disposed.

Subsequently, a few Malays joined the Japanese Volunteer Force, although it is unclear how many. Others slipped out of the country and enlisted with guerilla forces in the Peninsula. The Japanese also sent many Malays to Burma and Sumatra as labourers. And they kept a close watch on those who remained on the island.

At about the time they set about eliminating the soldiers, the Nipponese High Command rolled down Bukit Timah Road into town. The convoy was a noisy one, with the drivers tooting their horns and flying their flags triumphantly.

But that was the closest the Japanese came to a victory parade. The long march down the Peninsula and the battle for Singapore had claimed the lives of 3,000 of his soldiers, so Yamashita saw no need for a victory parade. Instead, he ordered a sombre ceremony for the dead.

The Japanese military set up their headquarters at Raffles College. Their first priority was to restore order and discipline on the island. They immediately introduced draconian laws with severe punishment for those who broke them. Theft became a capital offence. When the soldiers came across looting, they shot into the crowds.

In the first few days of the Occupation, however, the looters continued to take chances. The houses of the Europeans who went to the Padang, for example, were stripped bare. Pianos turned up in kampung houses. One man even saw someone walking away with a kitchen sink!

But the Japanese acted swiftly. Evidence of just how serious they were about these new rules became horrendously apparent. With their long swords, they lopped off the heads of Chinese who were caught looting and stuck the heads, the blood still dripping, on posts at busy road junctions and other areas where there was high human traffic. Many people remember the severed heads on poles outside the Cathay cinema and the old YMCA building.

In their continued attempts to woo the Malay and Indian population to their side, however, the Japanese often let off non-Chinese looters with a warning.

It was quite clear to Yamashita that the thin number of Japanese forces on the island would need to work together with the local population to keep the country running. However, he had a more urgent and over-riding mission in mind. He needed to ensure the safety of his men by eliminating any remaining anti-Japanese elements, in case they organised themselves and mounted a guerilla attack. Tsuji, the mastermind behind the successful invasion suggested a *sook ching*, meaning "purification by elimination", among the Chinese community, especially as the Chinese had dared to organise a local resistance through Dalforce.

Yamashita agreed to the *sook ching* and gave this job to the Singapore garrison commander, Major-General Saburo Kawamura. Colonel Masyuki Oiishi, the head of the dreaded Japanese military police, the *Kempeitai*, who set up headquarters at the YMCA, was ordered to work with Kawamura.

With their immediate tasks of rounding up the Allied administration and troops over, the *Kempeitai* moved quickly to implement Yamashita's order.

Oiishi had 200 fully trained *Kempeitai*, and another 1,000 young army soldiers under his command, mainly rough peasants who were draftees, not professional soldiers. Suddenly they found themselves in almost absolute control over nearly a million people and they lacked the discipline to control themselves. They were to be responsible for the worst bloodshed the island had ever seen.

In the next few days, the massacres began.

On February 17, the Japanese gave orders through the radio, loudspeakers and posters for every Chinese male between the age of eighteen and fifty to report at one of five designated points by noon on February 21.

Just to make sure the Chinese turned up, on the appointed day *Kempeitai* men rushed into houses and at gunpoint, herded entire families to the concentration camps.

It was a heart-stopping moment for seventeen-year-old Lee Kip Lin when a *Kempeitai* soldier burst into his house, ordered the family to pack food for three days and march to Changi Road with the rest of their neighbours.

At first, Lee, a student, was quite lost in the confusion. Only when his family cook somehow found a handcart was he galvanised to help them quickly pack the cart with whatever food and drinks they could find.

All the while, the *Kempeitai* kept shouting at them to hurry. Lee's family, who were quite well-off, left everything else behind and joined the others as they began the long march from Amber Road towards Geylang. The hapless procession continued slowly along Changi Road until they came to a house which the *Kempeitai* told them to enter. Several other families were already there. The new arrivals crammed into whatever space they could find and settled in with no idea of what the next few minutes, hours or days would bring.

This process was repeated over a period of several days throughout the island. In some areas, the *Kempeitai* were better organised. They isolated the men and sent the women, children and the infirm home. Then they systematically singled out those whom their informants said were involved in anti-Japanese activities, and sent the rest home.

Thirteen-year-old Tan Ban Cheng was herded with his family into one of the more organised camps, at a remote place in Paya Lebar. The march to the camp was an unnerving one. One Japanese officer had a habit of raising his revolver and shooting into the air every time the group slowed down.

"And we were also told not to make any noise. So it was a quiet and frightening sort of march to the camp. Nobody really considered it an occasion to chat. We kept very silent," Tan said.

The Tan family and their neighbours began their march at about seven in the morning. They spent twelve hours at the camp before they were released.

That evening, back at the Changi Road camp, the Lee family received a shock when a policeman turned up at the house where they were huddled with their neighbours and told the gathering that all males between the ages of eighteen and fifty were to report to the Telok Kurau English School around the corner, at three in the morning.

At two in the morning, the males left the house. They marched in the starlight of the early morning hours to an unknown fate. As they walked, they were joined by other men coming from other directions. Nearer to the school grounds, they found thousands of others walking towards the same destination.

The school field was soon packed beyond capacity with about 10,000 Chinese males. It became apparent that whatever they were there for, they were early. There was not a single Japanese soldier to receive them. Nonetheless, the thousands waited. They milled around nervously as the sky grew steadily lighter.

When dawn broke, many saw for the first time the size of the mammoth crowd. Thousands were gathered there. As it grew brighter and warmer, they grew more restless, hungry and tired from the lack of sleep. It was around eight or nine in the morning when one Japanese officer finally appeared, with a few others in tow. They dragged behind them "like a dog", a Chinese man with his hands tied behind his back. In front of the crowd, the *Kempeitai* started kicking the man about. The crowd watched in horror as the Japanese made the man kneel.

The word went around, "He's about to be beheaded. Don't look."

However, while the Japanese continued beating him, the man suddenly jumped to his feet and ran for his life. Some of the Japanese soldiers chased after him, but that was the last the crowd saw of him.

Their attention switched to the Japanese officer who climbed a small rostrum of sorts and started making a speech. An interpreter translated as the officer lectured the crowd for half-an-hour on law and order. Then the few Japanese soldiers began sorting the thousands of Chinese into separate groups.

First they called for traders and merchants to step forward. Some of those who were self-employed stepped up and were marched away someplace.

Next, the Japanese wanted civil servants to step forward. Taking their cue from the traders, the civil servants owned up and were whisked away. No one could guess the point of this exercise.

The hawkers were next. The Japanese sub-divided them into different categories, according to what they sold.

Finally, they asked for students. Lee stepped forward with his brother and they were promptly marched off to a nearby house where they were told to wait in the compound. Lee, his brother and the others, took shelter under the coconut trees and watched the Japanese continue their mysterious operation.

As they crouched in the shade under the lazy eye of a few Japanese guards, Lee and his brother watched the sorting out process come to some sort of end on the open field with many men still detained. From where he was, it looked as if those men had a long wait ahead of them. Meanwhile, the afternoon sun crept to its zenith and shone down mercilessly on those in the open field where there was no shade.

Lee and his companions began to get unbearably thirsty, but they did not dare risk the wrath of any Japanese guard who might catch them wandering off in search of water. Finally, Ong, a schoolmate of Lee's, volunteered to go around to the back of the house to look for water.

As the others watched anxiously, Ong tried to slip away. But a sentry spotted him. The boys watched in horror as the sentry called a few other Japanese soldiers and with their help, tied Ong down before hauling him away. Lee never saw Ong again. As far as he knew, Ong was killed.

Fearful for their lives and cowed by what they had

seen, the boys huddled in the shade of the coconut trees. Their only consolation was that they were not out there in the open field where the sun beat down mercilessly.

Then Lee witnessed a display of the human spirit that he would never forget. It was about three in the afternoon and the sun was at its most vicious. As Lee watched in disbelief, the womenfolk from a nearby Chinese village began ferrying buckets of water to the men in the field, in open defiance of the soldiers' orders.

One Japanese soldier became so furious at the sight of the women on their mercy mission that he rushed towards the men who were scrambling for the water and swung his rifle butt into some of them, kicking the others. Then he started in on the women with his rifle butt and vicious kicks.

Lee could not believe his eyes when the women, beaten and abused, continued bringing buckets of water.

Finally, the Japanese soldier, worn down by his brutal exercise in the sapping heat, caved in at the sight of the determined women, some of them hurt and bleeding, still walking past him with buckets of water for the parched throats of men they had probably never seen before in their lives.

As the sun set, the Japanese sent away some of the groups they had sequestered. But nobody came around to the compound where Lee and his brother were. It was close to 6.30 in the evening when a passing Indian policeman stopped at the sight of this motley group under the coconut trees.

"What are you still doing here?" he asked in English.

"We are here because no one has told us what to do. The sentry has gone off," one member of Lee's group replied.

The policeman looked puzzled. "Has nobody given you permission to go?"

"No, no one has come around."

The policeman looked thoughtful for a moment. Finally, he said, "I think you'd better go home."

The group did not hesitate. They bolted for home.

In the compound opposite Lee's, one of his distant relatives felt terribly uneasy at the sight of the different groups dispersing while his was still waiting for someone to come around. He turned to a friend and said, "We'd better get out."

The friend refused to budge for fear of what the Japanese might do to them if they were discovered leaving without permission.

"There's no point waiting. I'm leaving," Lee's relative said and darted off. He escaped, but he never saw his friend again.

In the midst of the thousands at Telok Kurau was a teenager with his father and siblings. His name was Lee Kuan Yew. Nobody guessed then that he was going to grow up to be the Prime Minister of Singapore one day, not even his father, Lee Chin Koon.

"My heart was going 'thup, thup, thup' all the time," said the elder Lee. "If they asked you to stand aside, you were finished. I thank God none of my children were taken."

In other parts of the island, other fathers were not so fortunate. War heroine Elizabeth Choy recalled how the Japanese allowed her father through at the Arab Street screening centre, but stopped her youngest brother. "He called out, 'Father, father, are you going to leave me behind? Why don't you take me along with you?' "

When his son did not return home later, her father was so distressed that he nearly lost his mind. His favourite son never did return.

Most of the men who turned up at the designated areas had no clue what it was all about; they were just following orders. Twenty-three-year-old Tan Cheng Hwee joined the long queue at Upper Cross Street in Chinatown in his singlet, trousers and slippers. He guessed they were "more or less going for an interview".

The queue began at the corner of South Bridge Road and Upper Cross Street. The men filed quietly into Upper Cross Street where they were asked simple questions by a Japanese soldier. Tan wondered why "some were told to go this way and some were told to go the other way".

Unknown to him at the time, it was at that point that the local informants singled out their victims. The difference between returning home safely or being taken to an isolated spot and shot had nothing to do with how he answered the questions, but everything to do with whether he was picked out by someone he did not know.

When Tan's turn came, the Japanese soldier asked him, "What is your work?"

Tan said simply, "I'm a clerk."

He was given a chop on his singlet and told to go. He left with a sense of relief, but still without a clue to how close he came to facing death.

Apart from those picked out by the informants, the Japanese also singled out anyone with a tattoo, which to them indicated secret society connections. Those who had a tattoo of five dots on the back of their hands were condemned to certain death as they were considered hard core communists.

At the building in Tyrwhitt Road which for many years was Victoria School, fourteen-year-old Soh Guan Bee watched the Japanese single out those in his queue who had a tattoo of any size.

First they checked the hands. The older Chinese had to take off their shirts too to show if they had any tattoos. Soh wondered if the man right in front of him who had tattoos all over his body would be singled out. He held his breath as the *Kempeitai* officer came up to the man.

The soldier didn't hesitate for a second. He told the man with the tattoos, "You go that side."

Then it was Soh's turn.

Thankfully, it was a painless moment. The Japanese officer checked Soh's hands, looked him up and down, gave him the coveted chop and dismissed him. He hurried out through the gate at the far end. As the gate closed behind him, Soh turned to look at those who remained. There were still thousands inside. How many would come out alive, he wondered.

As the purge continued, the *Kempeitai* rounded up teachers, reporters and intellectuals. All Chinese who had newly arrived from mainland China were suspect. Every Hainanese, especially, was in serious danger because the Japanese considered them pro-communist. In other areas, Chinese who could write English were singled out. Even those who had been cooks or domestic help for the Europeans were in jeopardy.

On March 3, a Japanese news agency report intercepted by Allied Intelligence said nearly "71,000 anti-Japanese" Chinese had been detained and that progress was being made in controlling "anti-Japanese Chinese... in *Syonan*".

Eventually, though, the Nipponese High Command realised that the purge was not getting them anywhere. The main resistance figures had already slipped away. Instead, thousands of innocent civilians were being slaughtered and the Japanese were earning the deep hatred of the entire population. The *sook ching* was also driving young embittered Chinese men into the jungles of Malaya to join the Malayan People's Anti-Japanese Army, a guerilla force hastily assembled by the retreating British forces with the help of the Chinese-dominated Malayan Communist Party.

Finally, Yamashita's deputy, Major-General Keishin Manaki, called off the "mopping-up" operations. The new focus of the *Kempeitai*, he ordered, was to be a more selective hunt for the main resistance figures.

The number of actual deaths from the exercise remains in dispute even fifty years later. The Japanese say that at most 5,000 people were killed during that period. However, a Japanese reporter, Hishakari Takafumi, who arrived soon after the surrender and was attached to the Japanese 25th Army Headquarters, revealed later that the military authorities expected to kill about 50,000 Chinese in the "mopping-up" operations. Singaporeans say the accurate figure is indeed closer to 50,000. One account of a massacre says the sea off Sentosa turned red with the blood of the murdered.

Which is the correct figure? It will require an exhaustive inquiry, and this has never been held.

While the *sook ching* was going on, the Japanese also squeezed the Chinese community for a cash "gift" of $50 million to be raised within a month as atonement for their anti-Japanese activities in Malaya before the war. The task of raising this hefty sum, $10 million of which was supposed to come from the Singapore Chinese, was given to the Overseas Chinese Association (OCA). The OCA was formed by prominent Chinese such as Lee Choon Seng and community leader Dr Lim Boon Keng, who were tortured by the *Kempeitai* and forced to cooperate under the threat of death.

By June 20, the OCA had raised only $28 million despite repeated extensions of the deadline. They had to make up the deficit with a loan from the Yokohama Specie Bank that was to be paid back within a year at six per cent interest. The OCA presented the $50 million in cash to Yamashita on June 25.

Rich Jews too were arrested and released only after they surrendered large sums of money. Yet, this was not enough to save them. Eventually all the Jews were arrested and detained for the rest of the Occupation.

The Japanese adopted a largely hands-off policy with the Malays as they had no wish to encourage Malay nationalism in a region where the Malays were predominant. Nonetheless, they did rub many of the Malays the wrong way by reducing the status of the Sultans in Malaya and outlawing polygamy. The much promised lower food prices under Japanese rule that was actively propagated in a Malay newspaper never materialised and the standard of living of the Malays deteriorated during the Occupation.

The Indians were actively courted by the Japanese because they had a clear agenda: to enlist them in the war against the British by supporting a common hope among them for the independence of India. The Indians who refused to cooperate had more to fear from their countrymen in the Indian National Army and the related Indian Independence League than from the Occupation army. Interestingly, it appears that the Indians' struggle to free their motherland was by and large viewed sympathetically by the Chinese and Malays and so collaboration with the Occupation army aroused little hostility.

Meanwhile, the Japanese formed the Malayan Military Administration (MMA) on March 2, more than two weeks after the surrender. All Malaya came under the MMA but its headquarters was in Singapore as the Japanese were interested in the island as a permanent colony. They declared Singapore the capital of the southern region of the Japan Empire and renamed it "*Syonan*", which meant "Light of the South".

The Japanese civilian administration, the *tokubetsu-si*, or municipal government, was under Mayor Shigeo Odate and his deputy, Kaoru Toyota. The *tokubetsu-si* took over some government departments and was also responsible for the Riau archipelago. However, the full staff strength of this municipal authority never exceeded twenty Japanese. As such, it was in constant rivalry with the military administration of Colonel Watanabe, also set up in March and known as the *gunseikan-bu*.

Mayor Odate had the honorary rank of General and was an experienced old hand at civil government, having gained valuable experience in occupied China. He did manage to overrule Watanabe at times. But as it was war time, by and large, Watanabe's military authority got the right of way most times.

It was Watanabe who brought in Taiwanese as interpreters because they were proficient in Hokkien. Koreans came as prison guards. The ruthless behaviour of these expatriate soldiers was to earn them a worse reputation than the average Japanese soldier, and their notoriety was rivalled only by the *Kempeitai*.

The work of the civilian administration was onerous due to the sheer amount of physical work to be done on the war-ravaged island. Municipal services had to be normalised as soon as possible. All utility workers were ordered back to work and in about six weeks the water supply was brought back to normal. It took about a month to put out the oil dump fires and the acrid smoke hung heavy in the air for weeks.

There were also dead bodies rotting everywhere, including several that washed up on Elizabeth Walk, as some Chinese committed suicide rather than give themselves up to be tortured by the Japanese. The Japanese were anxious to clear away the rotting bodies and gave this job to the civilians as well as the prisoners of war.

There were tonnes of debris on the island, but by April, the Japanese had more than 8,000 prisoners of war clearing the debris, repairing the roads and restoring the infrastructure of the island, especially the badly damaged docks. Each prisoner earned ten cents a day for his labour. Part of their work involved bringing down all the iron telephone poles and replacing them with wooden posts. The iron poles were shipped to Japan to be used as raw material for her ammunition factories.

Many prisoners volunteered to work as they got better rations and a chance to interact with the local population. This gave them opportunities to buy cigarettes and canned milk, and steal small amounts of food whenever an opportunity presented itself.

Doctors were told to reopen their clinics and what was left of the private medical health system was back in operation within two weeks of the surrender. Even British doctors and nursing staff were allowed to practise, at least until the conquerors could replace them with their own people from Japan.

All doctors were required to register with the authorities. The Japanese also registered Chinese *sinseh* or medicine men as qualified medical practitioners. Ho Yit Leong, then a young physician from a long line of traditional medicine men, suddenly found himself "promoted."

"Probably because there was a shortage of medical personnel and health facilities at the time," Ho explained. "Moreover, Chinese medicine has always been a part of Japanese tradition."

Ho received a certificate from a military commissioner permitting him to practise traditional Chinese medicine in Singapore and the Malayan Peninsula. He was not, however, allowed to perform dental surgery or administer anaesthesia and injections.

"To get the certificate, I went through a test which touched on only the rudiments of Chinese medicine," he said.

Meanwhile, the task of reshaping the island in the image of the Japanese continued apace. The master plan included eradicating all European influences and promoting the native lifestyle and languages in conjunction with the Japanese way of life. In practice, however, what emerged was not a partnership, but a master-servant relationship.

The statue of Stamford Raffles was promptly removed and the tower clock in the Victoria Memorial Hall building was reset two hours ahead so that it would keep pace with Tokyo. For the next few years of the Occupation, Singapore followed Tokyo time.

The Japanese promoted Shinto Buddhism and built a large number of such shrines, but they wisely respected other religions, allowing the various religious festivals to continue as holidays. Japanese officials even turned up on such occasions as they wanted to cultivate the religious leaders' support for their programmes.

Mayor Odate's team introduced profound changes in the education system to establish *Syonan* in the people's psyche. It was one of the first tasks on the new government's slate. But it was ill-equipped to make sweeping changes so it started with more modest aims.

In the first instance, it aimed simply to keep children off the streets. Schools reopened as quickly as possible, hampered by the fact that many of the school buildings had been commandeered by the military for other activities, including torture and interrogation of civilians. (Superstitious Singaporeans were to continue claiming that they saw ghosts in some of these old school buildings for decades to come.)

It took another four months or so for the Japanese vision of school education to take shape. It involved substantial changes to the British-style education system. The British had emphasised academic excellence, with athletic prowess seen as an extra-curricular activity. Due to the traditional British aversion to interfering in people's private lives, little or no emphasis was placed on moral education, except in missionary schools. The Japanese curriculum, however, emphasised universal moral education, physical training and working with one's hands in vocational training.

They made schooling an eight-year experience. Primary and vocational schools were given special emphasis. Odate managed to stave off Watanabe's drive to do away with English in the schools altogether and instead pushed Japanese as the main language at a more reasonable pace. He brought in teachers from Japan and introduced Japanese language classes on the radio and in the newspapers.

There were economic incentives for people to learn the Japanese language. Civil servants who picked up the Japanese language received bonuses and some were even sent to Tokyo for advanced Japanese language classes. These incentives worked about as well as could be expected, given that Japanese was not an easy language to pick up. Many teachers and students responded positively and most schools were using it as the main language of instruction by 1944.

However, parents were generally not too keen to send their children to schools where most of the day was spent on tough physical exercises, gardening and singing Japanese songs. The children did not seem to learn anything except to love the very Empire which had caused the disappearance of their uncles, aunts or immediate family members.

For their part, the Japanese made no secret of the

fact that the main emphasis of the education system was inculcating loyalty to the Japanese Empire. Every morning, schoolchildren faced the direction of Japan and sang the Japanese national anthem, Kimigayo, and other patriotic Japanese songs.

Showing a keen appreciation of the importance of mass communication, the new rulers of Singapore exploited the existing infrastructure to bring out their first newspaper here quickly.

This was a Malay newspaper, whose editors had been arrested earlier by the British for publishing Japanese propaganda. The editors were released and the paper appeared within two days of Singapore's capture, in both a romanised and Jawi version. The other newspapers were back in business within a week. The Chinese newspaper, Sin Chew Jit Poh, went under the name of *Syonan Jit Poh*.

The Straits Times became the *Syonan Shimbun*, which meant the Singapore Times. It became the official English daily newspaper and everyone was required to read it. It also acted as the official bulletin of daily orders from the Nipponese High Command to the people of Singapore. At the bottom of the page, it always carried a warning that failure to follow the orders would result in severe penalties, and everybody had enough reason to believe it. It was about the only thing in the paper they could believe.

To make it easier to communicate orders, the Nipponese High Command let everybody keep their radios, but they wanted them to be able to receive only their own propaganda broadcasts. Accordingly, the Japanese demanded that everyone who owned a radio surrender it for necessary "adjustments" and removed the short wave circuit.

To be found listening to a foreign broadcast was a severe offence. Nonetheless, some people dared to defy the authorities and kept a radio set in the house with the short wave circuit intact so they could receive the British Broadcasting Corporation broadcasts.

One of the most amazing stories from the war is an anecdote from L. A. Duckworth about a close shave he and his friends had infringing this rule: "We whiled away the long evenings with nightly sessions of bridge. During the sessions, my friend's radio would be tuned to the BBC's programmes, but on a very, very soft volume. One night, a foursome of bridge was on in the sitting-room. Also in the room, but fast asleep on the settee, was my friend's seven-year-old son, Jimmy. The radio was softly playing pop music.

"Then, with terrifying suddenness, and without warning, a Japanese official in full uniform, complete with long *Samurai* sword, appeared in the doorway. He was wearing rubber-soled shoes, which accounted for his inaudible footsteps as he mounted the front stairs. He stood in the doorway, coldly and superciliously surveying us. He ignored my friend's polite invitation to come in and take a seat.

"With cold shivers running down our spines, we went on playing bridge, guiltily conscious that within moments the radio would announce, 'This is London, here is the news!' To have got up and switched off the radio would have aroused suspicion. So we just carried on with the game — while the officer stood there and glared at us, saying nothing, which made it all the more menacing and alarming.

"Then suddenly, amazingly, just a few seconds before the familiar six pips would have heralded the BBC news bulletin, young Jimmy, who had, under strict parental prohibition, never before in his life touched that radio set, woke up in a sort of dreamy daze, walked from the settee to the radio and turned it off!

"Then, still in that seemingly somnambulistic daze, he ambled off to bed. When questioned the next day, he totally denied having switched off the radio!

"The relief of the bridge players at this startling anti-climax cannot be described. After a while, and still without saying a word, the Japanese officer, who was probably a snooper from the *Kempeitai*, turned on his heels and strode out. Four almost hysterically relieved bridge players shook hands and called it a night."

Such was the climate of fear. The battle for the hearts and minds of Singaporeans continued but was undermined by the harshness of the regime and its inability to deliver on its promises of cheaper goods and services, crippled as it was economically by rampant corruption and inefficiencies.

For example, although the declared intention was to make Singapore self-sufficient, it was never clear what steps were taken in this direction during the Occupation. Singapore's dependence on imported food meant she was particularly vulnerable, but the situation was worsened when large Japanese firms were given monopolies to produce different commodities, including rice and sugar. They, in turn, formed syndicates to control supply and jack up prices. Instead of boosting production, as soon as any syndicate got control of a commodity, it disappeared from the shelves and had to be bid for in the black market. Japanese firms proved the profit motive a stronger force than their loyalty to the war effort.

As for the hinterland that the Japanese hoped would supply their war effort with rubber and tin, production levels did not reach even half the pre-war levels. This impoverished people all around and affected Singapore's economy too. Those with a British education, holding white-collar jobs lost out. Even if they retained their jobs, a fixed salary was not very useful in a country facing severe shortages and rampant inflation.

They were joined in depression by those who steadfastedly refused to cooperate with the Japanese — and there were many — who managed by selling their possessions and drawing on depleting reserves, hoping that the British would return to save the day.

In the early months of the Occupation, the price of necessities shot up while luxury items plummeted in value as looters off-loaded quickly to avoid being caught with giveaway clues like expensive items in humble houses. By April of the first year of Occupation, the black market was firmly established as the shopping centre of the desperate — and everybody was desperate. Every time the Japanese authorities tried to suppress the black market with strict action, it only jacked up prices further.

As everyone was forced to trade on the black market, it became a respectable thing. Enterprise and the ability to make good was respected.

Ling Lee Hua, who was to become a prominent businessman in the post-war years, was only twenty years old when the war came, but managed to outwit his fate with his entrepreneurial skills. "Everyone was hunting for food, literally. I made a bit of money bringing together people who were willing to sell their tinned food or powdered milk and people willing to buy them. Just for fifty cents, I walked all the way from Race Course Road to Tiong Bahru to deliver a tin of powdered milk. If you had a good bicycle then, it was like owning a Rolls Royce today."

In the middle of the Japanese Occupation, Ling and his friends ventured into the ice cream business. They got together whatever amounts of milk and sugar they could find and made coconut-flavoured ice cream that they sold to restaurants. Ling made five cents for every twenty-five cent cup the restaurants sold.

"I usually managed to make a small profit, but on cool days when no one wanted to eat ice cream, it was a total loss and I had to eat the ice cream. I keep telling my grandson the money his toys cost is more than the capital I started the business with."

There was a lot of scope for enterprise. Transport was one area where a few made a living. As the Japanese had requisitioned most of the vehicles on the island, buses became the main form of transport and the only alternative for passenger travel was the three-wheeled contraption that today exists only outside expensive hotels for novelty rides — the humble trishaw.

Chia Kee Huat recalled how he lost his job at a rubber factory, but found himself a niche as a trishaw-rider.

"A trishaw-rider's life was not too bad then. Our only worry was meeting soldiers on the road. Some of them paid the fare, but others refused.

"It was worse near midnight, when I had to take them from the downtown shopping area to their barracks in Bukit Timah, Holland Road or Pasir Panjang where you could not expect to pick up passengers on the return trip.

"It was sheer bad luck if I met other soldiers on the return trip. They would order me to take them back to their barracks. There were nights when I made many trips until dawn — and all for nothing."

By the time the war ended though, Chia owned three trishaws, one for his own use and two which he rented out. Forty-five years after the war, he owned a metal container-making company.

While life was hard for the majority of the population during the Occupation, for one group of people, it became a crazy, hedonistic, live-for-today world. Those who were able to bribe their way into favour with the Japanese businessmen who held key licences for manufacturing or other production made quick fortunes, which they spent as easily as they made. They were the middlemen between those seeking favours and those with the power to grant them. So large a class did they become that they supported two or three gambling dens and entertainment places like Happy World. They gave a depressed country an air of rough gaiety at night.

Things were made worse when the Japanese introduced their own military currency, what people called "banana money" because of the trademark banana and coconut designs. When the Japanese offensive was doing well their currency was still sound, but when the tide of war turned against them confidence in their currency plummeted. To make things worse, the Japanese brought in small printing presses and started issuing bills without index numbers, making them easy to forge. Singapore was soon faced with a glut of such currency and in the later part of the war some transactions required wheelbarrows of notes!

The food situation deteriorated steadily during the Occupation, reaching crisis proportions towards the end. As the Japanese hoarded rice supplies for the war effort and other supplies from Burma withered, the shortage of rice became chronic. The Japanese response was to encourage people to grow their own food. They allowed people to make use of any vacant plot near their homes to grow vegetables. They even held gardening contests and gave small loans to small-time farmers and offered gardening tips. Vegetable farming became a school subject.

As food grew scarce, many people turned to innovating recipes to make do. Phua Cheng Kew was twenty-five years old and already a baker for five years when the Occupation began. He remembered the recipe for the coarse and bitter bread he made then, using palm oil as one of the ingredients.

"We had to use tapioca flour instead of wheat flour as supplies from Australia and Canada were cut off. It was a poor substitute. As tapioca bread lacked essential vitamins, people who ate it over a period suffered from beri-beri."

But these were patchworks to hide the real truth: the Japanese had squandered every opportunity to build bridges with the local population. They had few plans for any major improvements or to increase productivity, and were now facing a deteriorating situation, a slide into anarchy, as their rule by force failed to make unwilling hands produce the goods they so badly needed.

By 1943, things changed even in the theatre of war. The Japanese were facing heavy losses in battle as the Allies swiftly turned the odds against them.

In 1944, out of desperation, the Japanese tried to increase productivity by force. Their gardening tips turned into orders and they intimidated the make-do farmers with severe threats but failed to work any magic. Civil servants were sent to work on vegetable plots with little success, even when poor productivity was considered sabotage.

There was also a move to press the people of Singapore into an unwilling defence. Around May 1945, the Japanese began civil defence programmes for civilians. Men and women were called to the Padang for several military exercises. But these were listless attempts at engendering a resistance movement. The Japanese could not create a Dalforce of their own.

Even the volunteer military units that the Japanese did manage to organise from June 1943, such as the *Heiho*, *Giyu Tai*, and *Giyu Gun*, were not trusted with the defence of Singapore. Only the *Giyu Gun*, which was a regular volunteer army, was armed, and the only combat they ever saw was against communists in east Johor.

Then, in November 1944, the people of Singapore saw American planes roar over the island to attack the harbour.

The Allies were back in force.

Lee Tian Soo recalled, "Sometimes as we walked down the streets, we could hear the powerful American planes which flew very high up in the sky. When we looked up, we could see the Japanese planes struggling to climb high enough to engage the Americans. But they could never do it. The Japanese soldiers didn't like us seeing all this. If they saw us looking at the planes, they would shout, '*KURRAH*! *KURRAH*!', which meant 'Get Out!' They knew we were admiring the American planes."

The Allied air attack followed a very different pattern from the Japanese version almost three years before. After the initial attacks, they made a show of strength by appearing often, but limited their bombing runs. They did not want to cause too much damage because they were confident the Japanese would eventually capitulate and the facilities would serve the Allies again.

The planes instead concentrated on cutting supplies to Singapore, while the naval forces mined the waters.

They were quite successful in their efforts. Unfortunately, among the first casualties of the shortage of food and other supplies were POWs and civilians detained in the various centres. As food supplies dwindled, many of these prisoners starved to death.

Out in the streets, another group of people suffered the same fate. They were the thousands of Javanese men and women brought in by the Japanese en route to the railway works in Thailand. Some made it to their destination, but with the Allied bombing, most of the transients were stuck in Singapore.

Young Othman Wok witnessed hundreds of the Javanese literally starving to death by the roadside.

"Those with education worked with the Japanese. I knew two of them who became glass blowers. But those without education led a wretched life and many died on the roadside. No one cared because there was a hell of a lot of confusion towards the end of the war."

In many areas, essential services ground to a halt. Broken machines lacked spare parts. The hospitals ran short of medicine. The long queues of the Occupation days became even longer queues of emergency. Rice supplies were so low that people who dropped a little rice on the street bent down to pick up every grain. Those selling goods on the black market were the only ones who profited as prices soared.

The Japanese war losses became too obvious to hide by early 1945, the last year of the Occupation. They put about 6,000 POWs to work shoring up the defences of the island and Johor.

Despite the Japanese efforts to block outside news from reaching Singapore, many people were glued to their clandestine radios throughout the day. Events unfolded rapidly. The war in the European theatre closed in May and the Allies turned their attention to the East, soon recapturing Rangoon.

The news would have been even better received if the food and supplies situation in Singapore was not getting more critical by the day. The view that the Japanese would take everyone with them in a massive *harakiri* frenzy soon spread through the island and people became very anxious.

The Allies sent their planes over Singapore in daily sorties now. Over at the Bahau settlement in Negri Sembilan where the settlers were completely cut off from the world, George Bogaars watched the Allied bombers fly over them to bomb Singapore.

"Once they dropped some leaflets. It was news about the war that was going on in Burma. One of those 'Keep your spirits up' kind of leaflets," Bogaars said.

On August 15, those who were listening secretly to the BBC, heard the words they were longing to hear: The

Japanese had surrendered.

Syonan was not told of this immediately. The Japanese authorities kept the news under their hats for two days as they decided how best to handle it. Even their own men in the rank and file were not fully aware of the surrender.

Over at Japanese Naval Intelligence, a stenographer named Forest could not believe his eyes when he read the message that the Emperor of Japan had told his forces to surrender to the British. Looking out for anyone who might be watching him, Forest walked over to a typewriter and slipped in some paper. Quickly he typed out the message, and then, with one more look around to make sure he was not being watched, he folded the paper and slipped it into his shoe. When his shift was over, Forest went straight to the clinic of a close friend, who was a doctor.

Frank James, a teacher in St Joseph's Institution, was visiting that doctor when Forest arrived. James said, "On his face was an undisguised look of sheer joy. I realised that he had exceptional tidings that day. Sure enough, he drew out a typewritten notepaper and read to us exultantly the news of the Emperor's capitulation decree following the bombing of Japan."

News of the surrender spread rapidly by word of mouth for two days before *Syonan* officials finally declared it to the public. Even then, the official word was not that Japan had surrendered, but that the Emperor of Japan had decided to end the war.

Nobody was fooled.

Immediately after the announcement, inflation went through the roof. There was a mad rush for British currency.

The public had already noticed how some Japanese officials were suddenly rather pleasant. One witness said, "Our Japanese employers treated us with extraordinary courtesy. They gave us a lot of rice, sugar, cigarettes and $2,000 in banana currency — advance pay for three months."

Four days later, on August 21, the press reported Singapore's surrender. Suddenly, there was a short dip in the inflation rate as Japanese-run organisations dumped their goods at bargain prices before disbanding. All over the island, Japanese signs were torn down and Japanese flags burnt. Reading the writing on the wall, the ruthless Taiwanese agents who were interpreters for the Japanese forces and spoke fluent Hokkien, slinked away from their posts, blending in with the crowd. Some of the rich collaborators ran off to Hongkong. Many policemen and official lackeys also disappeared from their posts.

Most of the Japanese prepared a place of self-exile in Jurong, according to British instructions, and packed themselves away there, with only a few officials left to run Singapore. There was an unfortunate interim period of three weeks between the announcement of surrender and the arrival of the Allied troops as General Douglas MacArthur, the Supreme Commander of Allied Powers in the region, decreed that the Allies should not land on

Japanese-occupied territory until the enemy had formally surrendered to him.

During this period, looting was rampant again, reminiscent of the days of the Japanese invasion. The communist Chinese youth set out on a witch-hunt for collaborators and although Singapore did not suffer the blood baths that the guerilla forces caused in the Peninsula, guerilla bands did hold some kangaroo courts in the Geylang area and executed collaborators.

There was also some racial tension as the racial divisions exploited by the Japanese led to the killing of some Sikh watchmen and Malay policemen, but most of the collaborators escaped. Many of those who had joined the Indian National Army fled their camp in Bidadari and went into hiding.

Finally, the British returned in warships on September 5 as the crowds lined up on the seaside to watch, wave flags and welcome them back. The arriving officers made friends easily.

"Each time a British soldier visited his local friends, he came like a Santa Claus, with a bundle of tinned food and cigarettes and even liquor," recalled Lee Liang Hye.

On September 12, exactly a week after the Allies had returned, a large crowd assembled on the Padang. They jeered five Japanese generals and two admirals who led a delegation up the steps of City Hall to offer their formal surrender to Mountbatten. Standing with Lady Mountbatten at the ceremony was one of the representatives of the local population, Elizabeth Choy, a war heroine who truly suffered all the travails of the Occupation, including severe torture and a forced separation from her husband for nearly two years.

The Union Jack once again flew over Singapore though several young men of foresight who stood on the Padang that day anticipated, as they watched it fluttering in the breeze, that its days as a symbol of colonial rule were numbered.

Japanese torture methods

People will find it hard to believe that clean and green Singapore where the biggest complaint is that nothing very much happens was once the scene of extraordinary pain, torture, mutilation and massacre. Much of the horror occurred in places that we pass by everyday with not the slightest inkling of their tainted history.

Captured Japanese Intelligence documents revealed the extent to which they had refined their torture methods to achieve the best results.

A manual titled, Notes for the Interrogation of Prisoners of War, issued to the troops in Burma, included these instructions:

"Care must be exercised when making rebukes, invectives or torture as it will result in the prisoner telling falsehoods and making a fool of you."

The recommended methods of torture included "kicking, beating and anything connected with physical suffering. This method is to be used only when everything else has failed as it is the most clumsy. Change the interrogating officer after using violent torture, and good results can be obtained if the new officer questions in a sympathetic manner."

After the war, an inquiry by the British revealed the various methods used by the Japanese interrogators.

They included:

1. Beatings all over the body with iron bars, brass rods, sticks, bamboos, wet knotted ropes, belts with buckles, or revolver butts.

While these beatings were inflicted, the victims were sometimes suspended by the wrist from a rope passed over a beam. Sometimes their hands were tied behind their backs and they were forced to kneel on a sharp piece of wood or iron. At the same time, sharp-edged pieces of wood or metal were placed behind their knees to cut into their flesh.

While the victims knelt, the interrogators jumped on their thighs or on the projecting ends of the bar or the wood behind their knees. Sometimes, to increase the pressure on the bar or wood behind their knees, a soldier would perch himself on the shoulders of the victims. Or the victims, with hands untied, would be compelled to hold heavy weights above their heads.

The victims were often forced to remain in this position without intermission for nine to ten hours. During this period, interrogation would go on remorselessly, punctuated by blows. At times, the victims would be tied to a table and remained tied until they lost consciousness. This treatment was, in some cases, carried on daily for four to five days consecutively.

In one case, a European, who died later, was interrogated with the usual beatings for fifty-five hours at a stretch and another European, who also died, underwent a total of 144 hours of torture, according to the estimates of his cellmates.

2. Water torture: There were two forms of water torture. In the first, the victim was tied or held down on his back and a cloth passed over his nose and mouth. Water was poured on the cloth. Interrogation proceeded and the victim was beaten if he did not reply.

As he opened his mouth to breathe or answer questions, water went down his throat until he could hold no more. He would then be beaten over his distended stomach and often, an interrogator would jump on his stomach or step on it.

In the second method, the victim was faced upwards and tied lengthwise on a ladder, with a rung of the ladder across his throat. In this position, he was slid, head first, into a tub of water and kept there until almost drowned. After being revived, interrogation continued and the torture was repeated.

3. During interrogation the interrogator often burnt the victim with cigarette and cheroot ends, even on the most sensitive parts of the body, like the armpits, between the toes, on the scrotum and penis. Several prisoners had petrol poured on their bellies and ignited and one had his hands tied together and immersed in a bowl of methylated spirit, which was then ignited.

4. Electric torture. There were two types of electric torture. In the first, an induction coil was used, with one electrode attached to the hand or foot and the other, a bare wire, applied to various parts of the body.

One victim reported that he was thrown across the

room by the violence of the electric shock. The second form, apparently more severe, was called the electric table or electric cap.

5. In addition to these forms of torture, the interrogator often employed other methods such as twisting the limbs, bending back fingers, punching, repeated blows on the same spot and so on. These methods, in many cases, resulted in dislocations and permanent damage to limbs and joints.

In one case, the interrogator punctuated his questions by flicking with the frayed end of a bamboo at the victim's flesh, which was already bruised from a previous beating.

6. In several cases, the victims were led to believe that their execution, either by beheading or shooting, was imminent. They were advised to write a letter of farewell. Preparations for execution were carried out up to the last minute with such realism that in some cases the victims fainted.

7. Threats were also made against the families of the victims.

Torture was carried out to the limit of human endurance. One prisoner attempted to commit suicide by jumping off the verandah. In his fall, he fractured his pelvis but, despite his condition, his interrogation under torture continued until shortly before he died.

In another case, a prisoner pleaded with his interrogator for a gun so that he could shoot himself. A pistol was produced and snatched away only when the interrogator was convinced the man was about to shoot himself.

If the attack had come from the sea, Singapore would have been impregnable. But they came by the backdoor.

— War heroine Elizabeth Choy.

Australian soldiers building beach defences

Meeting Elizabeth Choy

Mrs Elizabeth Choy, born in Sabah in 1912, is an unusual woman in many ways, not just because she is one of the handful of Singaporeans whose war story has been told and remembered. Her experiences were documented in a play performed by TheatreWorks; a performance which brought back painful memories and made her cry.

Of all the people I interviewed, I was most nervous about meeting her; I am still not sure why. But when I saw her, I was stunned at how simple and unaffected she was for a person who has been written about so much and practically put on a pedestal. And she has such a warm, out-going personality that she put me at ease right away. She lives in a pre-war house that has a lot of personality, much like its owner.

Mrs Choy was dressed simply in a cotton shirt and old-fashioned tailored pants. Her hair was tied up in a simple bun, her bespectacled face filled with freckles, wrinkles and everything else that age brings. Yet when she spoke, she exuded great spirit and vitality and really was just very youthful. More youthful than a lot of people much younger than her. Having met her, and felt the strength of her character, I can understand how she survived the atrocities that were inflicted upon her.

Like the many others who spoke to me, it could not

have been easy for her to recall those horrible days, but she was most patient, her memory as keen as any person half her age. Often her voice shook with emotion, especially when she spoke of her family. Her story of how she sought in vain for news of her youngest brother, who was detained by the soldiers, made me cry.

Imagine a young woman trudging the streets during the Japanese Occupation, looking for her young brother, receiving kicks and punches from Japanese soldiers when she asked them what could have happened to him. Imagine a woman so gentle that in her own words she would not hurt a fly, tortured by the *Kempeitai* for helping to pass messages and food to the prisoners of war in Changi Jail. Imagine a woman burnt with electric charges while her husband was made to kneel in the same room and watch in despair.

These were only part of her many tribulations, not what a human being should be called upon to suffer in one lifetime. Yet when the time came for the reckoning, Mrs Choy refused to call for the hanging of her tormentors. Even today, her message continues to be anti-war, not anti-Japanese.

Mrs Choy began her teaching career at St Margaret's School in 1933, joining St Andrew's Junior School tutorial staff in 1935. Then came the war. After the liberation, she and her husband were decorated, and Mrs Choy went to Britain for rest and recuperation. She spent four years in Britain, studying spastic science and art, teaching in a London County Council School, even working part-time as a nude model for artists. She also went on a lecture tour of the United States and Canada, sponsored by the British Foreign Office.

On her return to Singapore, Mrs Choy became the island's first woman legislator, championing improvements in social welfare during her term from 1951 to 1955. She was a very different kind of politician. Fire victims found shelter in her MacKenzie Road residence; she adopted three young girls whose parents could not afford to look after them.

Mrs Choy's husband has since passed away and her three adopted daughters are grown-up. She has also retired from a teaching career at St Andrew's School that spanned forty years.

What keeps her busy now?

"My granddaughter," she says. Little Stephanie.

Clearly, in the twilight of her years, Mrs Elizabeth Choy remains focused on people outside herself. It is time to turn the focus on the lady herself...

I pinched the flesh of my thigh hard through my trousers... It was no dream.

— Mastermind of the invasion of Singapore, Colonel Masanobu Tsuji, on receiving news of the surrender of the Fortress.

British surrender to the Japanese

War heroine

Before the war broke out I was a teacher at St Andrew's School and my husband worked at the Borneo Company as a book-keeper. Financially, we were relatively well-off. We had two maids then because in those days help was easy to find and cheap. For $10, $20, you could get a maid. We had one to do the cooking and one to do the general cleaning. They were a necessity as I had a very large family to look after, you see, all my younger brothers and sisters.

In 1941 when there was talk of war, we were led to believe that Singapore was impregnable, and we believed it. When you think of it, Singapore's an island and the authorities expected the attack to come from the sea. There was an island, now called Sentosa, but at that time called Pulau Blakang Mati, which had all the big guns, all the ammunition. Ready for any attack. If the attack had come from the sea, really, Singapore would have been impregnable.

But unfortunately our enemy came by the back door, so there was nothing we could do about it. Our British soldiers were not trained for jungle warfare, and the Japanese were very good at it. They advanced from Thailand, down to Malaysia, and into Singapore. When they invaded Penang and we were told, "Oh, the Japanese are coming!", we still refused to believe Singapore could be overrun.

We said, "No, no, no, they've got no chance, no chance."

Right up to the end.

But when the Prince of Wales and Repulse came and both were sunk within a short while of their arrival, I was very sad, very depressed. I realised it would be extremely difficult for the British to hold out.

And the reality was becoming more apparent everyday. The shelling from the Japanese got nearer and nearer.

It kept going, "BOOM! BOOM! BOOM! BOOM!"
Continuously.

We had been told to prepare for air raids. But it was all very superficial. I suppose even the authorities were not expecting it. We were given sandbags and we also bought some of our own. We blackened our windows. We stored up on food like we were told to. But we were totally unprepared for the real horrors of war.

The bombing intensified to such an extent that schools had to be closed as it was no longer safe for the children to attend. St Andrew's School became a civilian hospital. The teachers were drafted into the medical service, either joining the Red Cross or the Medical Auxiliary Service (MAS). We had been given some training by the St John's Ambulance Brigade prior to that, so we became nurses, and tended to the wounded. I was in the MAS.

I remember the casualties jammed into the building.

They not only had to suffer the agony of their wounds, they also worried about the safety of their families. They went, "Oh, my family, I don't know what's happened to my family."

I had to console them, "Don't worry, don't worry."

But the sight I will never forget in this civilian hospital was that of an injured old lady. She was so badly hurt, her leg was almost severed from her body... she was in a terrible condition. I remember I said to the doctor who was attending to her, "If I should ever get to this state, just put me to sleep, please."

Although it was a civilian hospital, we did get one or two Australian soldiers who strayed into our compound. They were shell shocked. Poor things, they sat there and cried and as they sobbed, their bodies shook. It was terrible to see grown men behave like that. I prayed and prayed, you know, that there would never be any more war. It was just terrible.

At home in our MacKenzie residence, we had constructed a rudimentary air-raid shelter in the porch. The siren would go off every now and then, so towards the end of the war, most of the time the children and the old people huddled up in the bomb shelter. It was only about four by five feet and very cramped, so the rest of us hid under the beds or under the tables.

We also took in refugees. They were from Malaysia and had nowhere to go. They came to us and said, "Please, can we take shelter here?"

Of course we couldn't say no to them. We took

them in but there was no choice for them but to sleep on the floor. There were anywhere from ten to thirty refugees with us at one stage.

There were also some students from a boarding school called, Pudu English School, run by missionaries. Their principal had to go somewhere, and as Christians, we took the children in. In the end, though, we all had to flee. I don't know where they went eventually. Poor things.

We watched from our home as the Australian soldiers were shot at by Japanese aeroplanes. It was just up on the hill from my house, near Government House. Many of the Aussies fled down the hill and took shelter in our house.

We were educated in English, so of course our feelings were with the British and the Allies. We felt very sorry for them because they were fighting for us, you see. Our fate was their fate.

At some point, I remember the soldiers said, "Please, give us some tea."

We had some clean kerosene cans in which we made several buckets of tea. Oh, they were so thankful. And about six, seven years ago, one or two soldiers came back to thank us for the tea. It was so sweet of them.

By the time we realised that Singapore was going to fall, it was too late to escape. I had no thought of going away anyway because I had such a big family here. My mother had already passed away, but my father, step-mother, grandparents, brothers, sisters and nieces, were all in Singapore and we all lived together. There was no question of running away.

My father was about fifty at that time. He and my stepmother had come from Sabah to attend my wedding and my brother's wedding. We had a double wedding on August 16, 1941. My father and stepmother stayed on for a bit of a holiday and were caught by the turn of events. They couldn't go back to Sabah.

The shelling got worse as the Japanese moved into Singapore. They bombarded us so much that the back walls of our house collapsed.

We knew we could not stay in the house much longer. We hurriedly packed all the children and the old folk into the family car, an Opal Olympic, a German convertible. I remember the car well. I was very fond of it. You could cram a lot of people into that car.

We drove straight to Pearl's Hill, where there was a home for naughty girls. It was a solid building perched on top of the hill and a friend of mine was in charge of the place. I asked her, "Can we take shelter here?"

She said, "No, I'm afraid not. If I allow you to come, all the people will come."

I remember looking down on Singapore from that hill. All we could see was fire everywhere. Fire and smoke. It was terrible. As if we were in hell.

We didn't know what to do. We couldn't stay there so we just drove on. As we drove along Outram Road, fortunately, we were spotted by a friend, an Indian man who had a Chinese wife

He said, "Where are you going?"

We replied, "Oh, we don't know where to go. We're looking for shelter."

He worked in the hospital as a dresser or something. And my cousin had married a dresser there. So we asked him, "Where's so and so?"

He told us where to find my cousin, so we went there. She gladly took us in. "Come and take shelter with us. Don't go anywhere because the soldiers are coming down Bukit Timah Road," she said.

We stayed with her in the quarters in the General Hospital for one or two nights. People talked of the British surrendering. It was imminent.

When the Japanese took over Singapore, we watched from the window as the soldiers marched in. We thought the sky had fallen. That was the end.

Soon after, word got around that we were to report to Tanjong Pagar Police Station. There we listened to a barrage of propaganda, the purpose of which was to brainwash us. Through an interpreter, the Japanese warned us not to do anything anti-Japanese.

"You mustn't harm the soldiers," he warned.

After that, we were told to go to certain concentration centres. Women, children, the old, the young. Everyone of us had to go. The Japanese soldiers there looked very fierce and repulsive. We didn't take a liking to them, to put it mildly.

Our designated area was somewhere in Arab Street. They had cordoned off the area with barbed wire and the sentries were armed. We were there for about five days or so. It was hell. We were crammed into a building. You could hardly get food. The children were screaming. There was no water to bathe. Appalling conditions. Oh, it was a horrible time.

Finally, the children and women were asked to come forward and one by one as we passed through a gate, each of us got a chop on the arm to show that we had been screened. Only then were we allowed to go home.

But the older men and the youngsters were left behind. My father was released only towards the end and he had my youngest brother, Yong Chow Wee, with him. He was the youngest son, and very attached to my father — my father's favourite son. As Father walked past the soldiers to leave the camp, this young brother of mine followed, but was stopped by the soldiers. He was not allowed to follow my father out.

He called out, "Father, Father are you going to leave me behind? Why don't you take me along with you?"

When Father came home, he longed to see his son. He waited for my brother to return. Everyday, he looked out through the window. After one, two, three, four days, five days, a week passed and still there was no sign of my brother. My father was so distressed that he nearly went out of his mind.

I volunteered to go out and find out from the Japanese officers what had happened. As I walked along the streets, I saw other mothers, wives and womenfolk also wandering around aimlessly looking for their lost family members.

We didn't know what exactly to do, where to go or whom to ask. If we saw any Japanese soldiers, we asked questions and sometimes we got slapped. We got kicked on other occasions and were made to stand in the sun for hours. But still we persevered. The search went on for a long time, for weeks, with no results.

We heard rumours that the missing males were taken to Changi, where a big hole was dug and all the youngsters were lined-up around the pit and machine-gunned. All buried in one mass burial in one big grave.

But we were not satisfied. We continued to make enquiries. Until today, we still don't know what happened to my brother. He was seventeen. He was still at school. We have no idea why my brother was singled out.

From my family, three members disappeared or were killed at the hands of the Japanese: my uncle, a cousin and my brother. They were all young. Cut down in the prime of life. My cousin had just passed his final-year examinations at Raffles College. His mother nearly went mad when he disappeared.

My uncle, who was about thirty years old, was an operator on board a ship. They probably thought as he knew how to pass messages, he was dangerous.

When the Japanese moved in, my husband and I were left without any jobs. We had a family to support and no income. That was why we started a tuck shop at the Woodbridge Hospital. All the patients from the General Hospital were moved there when the Japanese overran the country.

You see, they had no canteen, no shops to cater for the influx of so many people. And when they wanted a cup of tea, coffee or a sandwich, there was nowhere to get it. We knew a lot of the doctors, nurses and so on. They knew that we had no jobs, nothing to do, so the chief medical officer said, "Why don't you come and start a tuck shop in our hospital?"

So we began by providing simple snacks. We had to buy food on the black market at whatever prices we were offered. It was a common practice during the Occupation as food grew increasingly scarce. Even tapioca was not easily available.

It was at this tuck shop that we became go-betweens for the people on the outside and those interned at Changi Prison. It just happened naturally. We saw their suffering and we wanted to help as best we could.

From time to time, sick prisoners were brought to Woodbridge Hospital. The ambulance driver was British and the doctor too. There was only one Japanese sentry to guard them. When the doctor took the patients to the ward, the driver would ask permission to come to our shop to buy something. There we would pass him the things. Sometimes it was money, sometimes food.

We wanted to help the prisoners also because so many of them were friends. The Bishop, Leonard Wilson, collected money on the outside, and gave it to us to pass on to the driver. The driver would then pass it on to the prisoners.

Another way that things were smuggled into Changi was through Norman Coolsen, an engineer who was allowed out of Changi to see to the maintenance of the Waterworks. Sometimes he would be asked to return to Changi with pipes or hoses for maintenance work. The Bishop stuffed money he had raised into those hoses.

Some of the people involved in this scheme like the driver, John Long, were later executed. And Doctor Boyer, who used to bring in the sick prisoners, died in the internment camp after he was arrested by the *Kempeitai*.

On October 10, 1943, the day that became known as the Double Tenth, the Japanese raided the prisoners' quarters and discovered hidden radios. They conducted a thorough investigation and they linked my husband and I to the whole scheme that they said was planned to topple them. They must have come to the conclusion that if the doctor and the driver called at our place, we had to be involved.

One day some Japanese soldiers came to our tuck shop — by this time we had moved to Tan Tock Seng Hospital — and asked my husband for directions to a certain road. My husband gave them the directions, but they claimed they weren't sure and asked him to go along with them to show them the way.

That was it. He didn't come back. By that time everybody knew that if you'd lost somebody like that, he was sure to be held at the *Kempeitai* Headquarters at the YMCA. So like a fool, where angels fear to tread, I rushed in. I went to the *Kempeitai* Headquarters and asked them what had happened to my husband.

At first they said, "No, we don't know."

I persisted, "He's not very strong, and he's got no blanket, no change of garment. Can I bring him a blanket?"

"No, no, no, no. We don't know what person you are talking about," they said.

But a week after that, the soldiers came to my house and said, "You said you wanted to see your husband. You wanted to bring him a blanket. All right, you come. Bring a blanket."

So I took a blanket and left with them for their Headquarters. A soldier escorted me into an office and told me to put my handbag down, take off my ring, this, that and the other. They took everything and led me to a cell.

I had long hair then and it was very important for me to comb it. I would brush my hair about ten times a day. When they told me to leave everything and I knew they would take me to a cell, my first instinct was to take out my small comb from my handbag and stick it into my hair that was knotted into a bun. But this blessed Japanese soldier walking behind me saw my comb and took it away. I went into the cell with nothing. No toothbrush, no change of garment, no comb, no soap, nothing.

I didn't know what to do. I was numb. In a daze. I still did not know where my husband was.

There were twenty men inside this tiny cell that they put me in. Some Europeans, Chinese and a few Malays. I was the only woman. At one point, there was another woman, but she was there for only a few days before she was taken away.

In the cell, there was a kind of raised platform. We had to kneel on it from morning to night. We were not allowed to stand up. There was a sentry watching over us all the time and they kept a strong light burning continuously outside our cell. When it was time to sleep, we rolled over and barely had enough room to stretch out.

There was only one commode, a lavatory in the corner of the cell. You had to do everything there. You washed your face there, you drank from it, you passed your motion there. No question of bathing. How to bathe there? There was no change of garment. All those men. No privacy. I don't know how I passed those days, you know. As a Christian, I prayed and meditated and put my trust in God. I believed that he would deliver me one day or at least give me the strength to bear my trials and tribulations. All the time, though, there was a song that played in my mind. Loch Lomond.

"For you'll take the high road, and I'll take the low and I'll be there before ye..."

I don't know why that song stuck in my head, but it kept me going.

After the war, when the Red Cross sent me to England to recuperate, I made it a point to go and see Loch Lomond. And when I saw Loch Lomond, I went down on my knees and took three handfuls of water to drink and sang that song to the lake. It was really an emotional moment. Even today, that song plays in my head.

But really I don't know how I managed to pass those days at the *Kempeitai*. I was in those appalling conditions for more than 200 days. No change of garment, nothing. No toothbrush, no comb. No soap.

We were on a starvation diet. After six months, my waistline shrank from twenty-five inches to fifteen inches. I could put my hand around my waist.

The hunger... unless you've gone through it, you won't know what hunger is. We always say, "I'm hungry"; all right, you can immediately get something to eat or you know there's something to eat. But when we were there we were really hungry. There's no word to describe it. All the time, we were thinking of food.

The only time you left the cell was when you were interrogated. There was a little gate that you crawled through. You went upstairs where they interrogated you and then they sent you back. You weren't allowed to talk to your cellmates, but somehow we learnt a sign language. When the sentry was not looking, we used it to communicate. Otherwise we would have gone mad, you see. We used our fingers to indicate the letters of the alphabet and till today I've found it useful in teaching the deaf and blind.

There was one particular Japanese officer at the *Kempeitai* who was extremely brutal. His name was Mona. He was a very handsome, very good-looking man. But he could be very, very, very terrible. He was only one of the officers who interrogated me, but he stands out in my memory.

One day, while interrogating me, suddenly he started joking with me, talking to me in a very friendly way. So I also spoke to him in a friendly way. Then, all of a sudden (Mrs Choy abruptly replays the scene when she was slapped), Bang! Bang! Bang!

I stared at him in shock. I was so humiliated, so insulted. I was never more angry in my life. Even when I was tortured, I never became as angry as that one time. I wouldn't answer him after that. He knew I had guts in me. Some dignity. I consider that the worst experience I had at the *Kempeitai*.

Although in terms of pain, the worst I experienced was when I was made to kneel on a three-sided log. I was tied up. I tried to go forward, backwards, sideways. I couldn't. Goodness, I was just rooted to one spot. I was made to strip topless on this frame. And they brought in my husband to watch me suffer. He was made to kneel beside this frame.

And we were told, "All right, you confess to this, that, and the other."

We were accused of conspiring to sink some Japanese warships or something. But we knew nothing about it. Then they said, "Tell us who were involved in the tuck shop scheme."

We said, "We know nothing. We only helped out of pity, we didn't do anything against the military."

The interrogators wouldn't believe us. They said, "Why are you so stupid? Why do you want to risk your lives to save the British? Tell us the truth and we'll let you go. We'll spare your lives."

We said, "We are telling you the truth!"

Then they threatened, "We will execute you if you don't tell us who were involved."

When we still stuck to our story, they said, "All right. You say goodbye to each other. Tomorrow we'll take one of you to Johor Baru to be executed. And the following day we'll take the other."

So I said, "All right, we'll say goodbye. We'll die an honourable death for the truth. We are not afraid to die."

Then they started to use electricity on me. Oh, it was terrible. I couldn't move. Tears were running down my face. My nose was running. It was terrible. I wanted to blow my nose, but I couldn't. Oh, that was the worst experience, really.

My poor husband. He had to watch me go through that. After that, I fainted and they had to carry me down. We really thought they were going to execute us.

But they didn't. They continued to interrogate us.

After six months, when they found I still maintained that I helped the internees simply because they were in need, the *Kempeitai* went around and asked people who knew me, my neighbours and so on, what I was like. They asked if I was anti-Japanese.

People said, "Oh, she's very kind, always willing to help others."

So one day, I was called to the office of a senior Japanese *Kempeitai* officer. He said, "Now you can go home. We have finished our investigation. We made enquiries and everybody we spoke to said you are really a very kind and helpful person. We know now that what you did was out of concern. We know that you are not anti-Japanese."

About three weeks before I was released, some of these officers went to my house and said, "Bring some food for Mrs Choy."

So everyday they brought me food. They wanted to build me up before releasing me.

I asked my father after my release, "How did you feel when the Japanese took me away and you didn't know where I was?"

He said, "I knew that no power on earth could help you. Nobody could help you. We didn't know where you were. But I believed that if it was at all humanly possible for anyone to get out of that place alive, you could do it."

I thought that was a great tribute from my father. He knew that I had great faith in God.

After my release I found a job as a cashier in a restaurant at Finlayson Green that was patronised by Japanese soldiers. I had to be very careful there because if I did anything wrong, it could jeopardise my husband's life.

My father took the family to Endau; he had no choice. The Japanese "encouraged" him to go. And my poor stepmother conceived her only child there. When it was full-term, there was no hospital there and I think there was trouble in the area too. Fortunately she was brought by lorry to Kandang Kerbau Hospital where she had a caesarean under local anaesthetic. The baby girl she delivered has grown-up to be a successful boutique owner who shuttles from New York to Paris and Rome, buying dresses.

We heard all sorts of rumours before the Japanese surrender. Finally, we could just sense it in the air. When the British returned to Singapore, oh, I cannot describe the joy I felt. I couldn't believe that we had survived all that. My husband was in Outram Jail, so one British officer went with me to get him out. When I saw my husband, it was like a dream. Like we were reunited in heaven in the afterlife.

I was invited by Lady Mountbatten to the surrender ceremony at City Hall and I attended that historic occasion. Then I went with her to Indonesia to do some Red Cross work. That's why the Red Cross later sent me to England to recuperate.

After the war, the British asked me, "Do you want those that tortured you to be executed?"

I said, "No. They are just ordinary people like you and I. They have families and they care for their families, for their children. They behaved like that because of war. I'm not against those who tortured me. I am against war. So let's work together for peace. During peacetime, these soldiers wouldn't have behaved like that."

The Japanese soldiers couldn't go against their superiors. How could they? If you were told to go and do this or that thing, would you go against your officer? If you are a soldier, you have to obey your officer. So the thing is to let there be no soldiers, no army, no nothing. Only peace.

I told the British officers, "I am forgiving, I want to forgive. Let's work together for universal peace, so that there will be no war. That is the answer."

But I think Mona was executed, because all the others wanted him executed. He tortured others too. And the other officer who was executed was Masuki, or something.

The scars of those days are still with me. I have a fear of all electrical gadgets for one thing. I refuse to learn how to operate them. I just can't cope with them because of the tortures I had to endure.

But since I never expected to be alive today, now I feel that I can't possibly go through anything worse than what I encountered during the war and neither can things be better than what I experienced after the war. I have led a full life and anything that happens now cannot possibly make me reach those levels of despair and elation that I experienced then. I went through the worst and the best. And now nobody can harm me except myself when I'm being selfish or unjust.

When they put up a play about my experiences awhile back, one young girl said she envied me because I had the opportunity to show patriotism and bravery. Having gone through the experience, though, when I think of the tortures, the degradation, and the insults, it still frightens me.

If you were to ask me if I would like to go back in time and go through that again, I would say, "No, thank you, a thousand times." But when you are confronted with such a situation, somehow you have to sum up enough courage to go through one tribulation after another. Having done it, I am thankful that I went through it with honour and love, but if you asked me to go through it again, please, no.

The Chinese were made to kneel. I watched as they were mowed down by gunfire.

— A Chinese farmer who witnessed one of the massacres at a village near Changi Road.

Evidence of a mass grave uncovered after the war

The Chinese massacres

The biggest blot during the Japanese Occupation was the island-wide *sook ching* or "purification by elimination" — the massacre of thousands of Chinese civilians on the grounds that they could be anti-Japanese elements.

While the exact number of casualties remains disputed to this day, Colonel Sugita, the head of Japanese Intelligence and the man who drafted Yamashita's surrender offer to Percival, testified that the Japanese murdered at least 5,000 people. Singaporeans believe the true figure to be closer to 50,000.

The massacres occurred between February 18 and March 3, 1942.

The first lot began when a Lieutenant Hisamatsu took over Tanjong Pagar Police Station with his *Kempeitai* troops and 100 other soldiers attached to his unit. His soldiers assembled the Chinese males in the area at three places: Tiong Bahru, the junction of Cantonment and Neil roads and the Harbour Board coolie lines. Large numbers of them were interrogated before they were shoved onto lorries and taken to the Tanjong Pagar wharf. There they were beheaded. This went on for several days and many headless bodies turned up on the beach of the Yacht Club.

On other occasions, motor launches took Chinese civilians, many of them Harbour Board employees, to a point about a mile off Sentosa where they were pushed overboard and shot. At least 150 bodies were washed ashore on the island.

There are eyewitness accounts from Singaporeans of massacres that occurred on the beach near the Chinese Swimming Club, a hill near the seven-and-a-half milestone on Siglap Road, Changi Beach and the beach at the end of Punggol Road, among other places.

The last of the biggest massacres was believed to involve 300 victims who were mowed down by machine-gun fire at a village near the 10th milestone on Changi Road.

A Chinese farmer described the massacre at the trial of seven Japanese officers: "In the early afternoon, I saw two cars pass my house, one with a red flag and the other with a blue one. Some Japanese soldiers got out and examined the air-raid shelters which were at the end of a lane at the rear of my property. Then they left.

"Two hours later, six or seven lorries full of Chinese civilians guarded by Japanese sentries went by the house and stopped at the air-raid shelters. The Chinese were made to kneel down in front of the trenches. I watched from behind a mango tree as they were mowed down by machine-gun fire. I heard them fall as they were hit and I heard the moaning of those who were not killed outright. The Japanese left soon after.

"I visited the place some days afterwards. The bodies had been covered lightly with earth, but it had not been done properly, and the stench of rotting bodies was so strong that we farmers reburied the dead."

In March 1947, the Allies tried and convicted Lieutenant-General Nishimura, Major-General Kawamura and five other officers on charges of being involved in the *sook ching*.

Kawamura and one other officer were hanged. The others were sentenced to life imprisonment.

What follows in the next few pages is a first-hand account by a man who survived a massacre, Mr Chan Cheng Yean.

We thought if we became prisoners of war, the Japanese would give us *makan*. We never thought they would kill us.

— Chan Cheng Yean, the lone survivor of a massacre.

Japanese soldiers shooting Sikh prisoners of war

Meeting Chan Cheng Yean

Mr Chan Cheng Yean, born in 1918, still walks around with fragments of a bullet in his leg. It was meant for his heart.

He survived a Japanese massacre.

Mr Chan is a very soft-spoken man, with very gentle and gracious manners, whose long years show on his face and his frame. He does not strike you as the kind of man who likes action movies featuring the likes of Chuck Norris and Sylvester Stallone, yet he does not miss a single one if he can help it. It sounds contradictory for a man who came so close to losing his own life in a massacre that for several months after he was by his own description, "crazy".

"He lost his mind," said his wife, who joined us during the interview.

Mrs Chan, a very animated and personable woman, was in Malacca at the time of the Occupation, living with Mr Chan's family. She had her own close call with the Japanese when drunken soldiers raided her house, looking for women to rape.

In her own words: "One night a spy brought three Japanese men to our place and caught hold of all the young girls. I was seriously ill, with typhoid fever. When they held me, they thought I was dying. So they didn't want me. They kicked me and hit me with their rifle butts.

"Then my husband's sister and my niece, two of them, were carried away. The Japanese took them to a graveyard nearby and wanted to rape them, but fortunately both of them had their periods. The soldiers kicked the two girls and left."

Today, these two extraordinary folk live a very ordinary life. I thought the most poignant comment Mr Chan made was towards the end of the interview when I asked the man who had a first-hand experience of a Japanese massacre, "Did the British ever contact you for the war trials?"

"No," he replied. "We are small fries."

One man survives a massacre

My uncle was a very clever man who had his own business in Malacca, where I worked as a clerk. He was also a captain in the Malacca Volunteer Corps. It was under his influence that I joined the Corps.

At that time, all the youngsters liked to be in the Corps, although you got no pay, you got nothing. You just served the British for the fun of it. You see, we liked the uniform they gave us and the prestige that went with it. It was just like an army, with ranks from private to major. There was some training; you learned how to drill, how to use a rifle. Once a year, they had one week of in-camp training. It was good fun. We even got a transport allowance.

When the Japanese invaded Malaya, the British declared Malacca an open city. We were not asked to defend it. The British did not have enough troops to put up a fight there. The Australians stationed there left too and the Japanese just walked through.

What the British did instead was to order all the volunteers from Malacca and Penang to defend Singapore, under the Straits Settlements grouping. However, except for one lieutenant, not one Penang volunteer responded. They knew that we could not win this war. People in Malacca were not as smart. Anyway, there was no choice.

Although we were volunteers, when war was declared, we became conscripts. If you refused to go, you could be charged as a deserter. Well, that was what I was told.

We were given helmets, uniforms, everything. We even had our own guns. But we never expected to be in a war. When we joined the Corps, it was for fun. We were young...

We arrived in Singapore by train and put up at St Patrick's School for three days. Then they transferred us to the Jalan Eunos Labourers' Camp. It became the head-quarters for the 4th Battalion from Malacca. It was actu-ally quarters for labourers employed by the government but when the bombing started, the labourers fled and so they stationed us there.

There were more than one thousand of us from Malacca, of all ranks up to major. The Corps was spread out in key parts of the island. Part of the battalion was in charge of the HQ in Beach Rd. Another group was at Fort Canning. The remainder in the camp, myself included, were sent out to the front line.

The British didn't trust us, so they put their own man in charge, Captain Todman. He was the officer com-manding us, the B Chinese Company. Our own Chinese officer, Captain Cho Seow Lim, became the second-in-command. We had two lieutenants: one of our own and the other from Penang, who had nowhere else to go. I was a private. I was only twenty-four years old.

On February 11, about twenty-five of us were moved to the front line and stationed under Captain Todman. We were the last line of defence, behind Cluny Hill, positioned between a battalion of Australian soldiers and a fighting force from India.

We learnt a lot about the Australians when we were there. They were the ones who didn't like to use helmets. And in the night, even though we told them, "Don't smoke," they always smoked. It was a dangerous thing to do because the light from the cigarettes gave the Japanese a clear indication of where we were.

But the Australians said, "Oh, that's better, we want to see them. They're hiding so we don't know where they are. This way we'll draw them out."

They were always like that, happy-go-lucky. They took the whole thing very lightly.

We, on the other hand, were very sad when we were sent up there. We didn't know how long we were going to be there. In the night, we heard gunshots in the area. It was very confusing. We didn't know who was shooting at who. The noise and the confusion was unforgettable. On top of that, they pounded us relentlessly from their aeroplanes during the day. The British had absolutely no air cover for us. How to fight such an unequal battle? We stayed put in our trenches.

Later, we were told that the Japanese soldiers were moving around in civilian clothes. They were even using sarongs and passing themselves off as Malays. So we received orders to shoot to kill anyone passing through our area who did not reply to our challenge.

We were told, "Just say, 'Stop, who goes there?' "

If they didn't reply, we were to shoot.

It was a battleground. Those were the orders. If anybody tried to cross, we shot. We couldn't see in the dark anyway. And it was the first time we were trying out our guns. Whether we hit our targets or not, we didn't care.

The Japanese made matters worse by camouflaging themselves so well. They made their move only under cover of darkness. They would climb up the trees and take pot shots at us. That's how they killed many of us. They dared not come out in the open. If they came openly, we would have fought them one to one. But they chose to do it differently and we had no answer to their tactics. So on our side, morale was low.

On the second day, we were shelled hard. The Japanese were using howitzers and trench mortars. We lost a corporal and a private in that assault. Later, Captain Todman told us that we had lost Captain Cho. After that, another private was killed.

Finally, after four days of relentless bombardment from the Japanese, we were told to withdraw. We retreated to a new position on the last day before the surrender. The order to cease fire was given at 2.30 on Friday afternoon, the fifteenth.

We had surrendered.

But the Japanese continued shelling us until about 4.30 pm. When the shelling finally stopped, we sat around, dazed, each one thinking about his own future. They had got us by surprise, the Japanese. The British had underestimated their military power, and their fighting tactics were far superior.

Some of us were thinking of making a run for it. Why should we sit around and wait to be taken prisoner? But we could not. Our superiors were still there, you see. The sergeant and our lieutenant said, "You'd better not run, there'll be trouble."

I said, "What trouble? Now finish, what? The British have surrendered already, why can't we run away?"

But on second thoughts, if we ran, where were we going to stay? We had no money. We did not know the city. We decided it would be better to become prisoners of war because they would give us *makan*, and all that.

We never thought they would kill us.

We waited for the Japanese to show up so that we could surrender to them. My captain would surrender to their captain. That was the proper way. We fell asleep uneasily that night.

The next day, after receiving instructions, we surrendered ourselves. We went to Bukit Timah Road where the Japanese military police, who were wearing arm bands, took us prisoner. They told us to throw away our weapons, grouped us and marched us to the Raffles College grounds. We were not afraid of them. We were following orders to surrender and they were taking us prisoner, that's all. Everybody was just following orders.

Those in the Corps who were at the Bukit Timah post and the Fort Canning post, they were lucky. When the British surrendered, the Corps members there were given $50 each. The British said, "Okay, throw away your uniform. If any of you have any relations, go and stay with them."

The British told them to go because they knew the Japanese would capture them. We got nothing on the front line. They could not contact us.

We were kept at the Raffles College grounds for three days. Soldiers from all the different battalions were there, even the British. We spent the time just walking around. They didn't give us anything to eat, but fortunately we had our own rations: biscuits.

After that, the Japanese moved us to Farrer Park where they had gathered all the Asian soldiers. Our British officer, Captain Todman, was on his way to Changi.

Farrer Park was such a large area and we were so many that we outnumbered the Japanese. That was our best chance to make an escape. Security was so poor that even the civilians came around, mixing with us, selling things for the dollars we had.

We should have made a run for it. One group of Eurasians did. Their Captain led the escape. They were smart, they seized the chance. We had no leader. Only conflicting ideas amongst us. Our European captain was in Changi, our Chinese captain was dead, and our sergeant did not know what to do.

There were many Indian soldiers with us. The Japanese came for them on February 22 and took them away somewhere.

Finally, on February 28, the Japanese came for us

at about nine in the morning. We lugged our belongings and marched from Farrer Park, through Geylang Road to Tanjong Katong Road where we were ordered to stay in a Chinese school that served as a Red Cross hospital during the invasion. We were a mixed group: Malays, Eurasians and the twenty-three Chinese volunteers from Malacca, plus a Eurasian who joined my group. I asked him, "Why didn't you run when you had the chance? Even your Captain said you could run! We cannot run because of our sergeant."

He said, "I've got no place to stay so I thought I'd better join you."

We waited with uncertainty. It was nearing sunset when the Japanese returned. They ordered the release of all the Malays, with the exception of their five officers. All the Eurasians were detained.

At about six o'clock, the five Malay officers, the Eurasians and the Chinese were marched to a house opposite the school. There, we were searched thoroughly. Then they tied our hands behind our backs and ordered us into three lorries. There were about ninety of us.

It was dark, about seven or eight o'clock when we reached Changi Road. We were ordered down from the lorries and told to climb a hill, which faced the sea. Now there is a big Housing Board block where this scene occurred.

The Japanese took us up to the trenches in batches. As one group went up, the rest of us waited by the lorries with a Japanese standing guard over us. We could hear

153

shots, but there was nothing we could do.

Then it was my turn. There were twelve in my group. The Japanese marched us up the hill with our hands still tied behind our backs. They took us to a British air-raid shelter and told us to surrender everything we had: money, valuables, even our watches. They left us only our uniforms.

Then they ordered us into the trenches. Those who hesitated were pushed in.

We stood there in the trenches, the twelve of us, facing a Japanese firing squad of twelve — one Japanese for each target. We were shivering in fright.

I realised I was facing death, but I did not give up hope. I prayed to the spirit of my dead father for help and offered my prayers to the gods.

Then the shots rang out. The Japanese soldiers fired three rounds into our trench.

By God's grace, only one bullet from the last round hit me in the leg. But on an impulse, I grabbed my comrade in front of me and fell into the trench with his body. Then another comrade fell on top of me. He was dead.

The danger wasn't over yet. The firing squad let off another round of bullets at the bodies in the trench just to make sure. I pretended to be dead. I didn't move a muscle. The slightest movement and I would have given myself away. My body was covered by a fallen comrade, but my head was exposed within the heap of bodies. I held my breath as the Japanese soldiers came forward. I kept my eyes closed and listened to the sound of their footsteps.

They came closer and stopped.

I was terrified.

In my heart, I prayed to my father, who had passed away two years ago. I prayed to him and to the gods. Please help me, please help me. Make them spare me. Do a miracle. Do a miracle.

And a miracle occurred.

The footsteps went away.

They moved to the next trench where another batch of prisoners waited. The same thing happened there. Three rounds of shots were fired and then, a last round to make sure. They went to the third trench and repeated their routine. This went on for about half-an-hour before silence fell.

I still did not dare move, and it was just as well because without warning, I again heard the sound of boots. Then there was a loud "BOOM!" They had covered my trench with a large plank. They had no time to even bury us. Perhaps they were planning to come back for our bodies later. I heard them put planks over the other trenches too.

The soldiers laughed and shouted as they went away.

I stayed in that trench with my dead comrades for about an hour or so. There was nothing I could do to save them. They were all dead. I was the only survivor.

When I thought it was safe, I moved the comrade who had fallen on top of me, and tried to climb out of the trench. But my leg was entangled with the other corpses. I wrenched it out and grit my teeth against the pain. I took one last look at my fallen comrades. I also checked the other trenches.

They were all dead.

I wanted to run away as fast as possible from that scene of slaughter but I was hit near the knee. There still are fragments of the bullet in my leg. I can use my leg all right today, but sometimes I feel the pain badly.

My leg was covered in blood, not just from my wounds but that of my comrades too. I made my way down to a drain where I washed the wound and then escaped to a nearby rubber estate. I found a patch of *lallang* where I could lie down and hide. That was my bed for the night.

Early the next morning, before the sun came up, I went looking for help. I was in extreme pain, hungry, tired and scared. Somehow I managed to make it to an area around Chai Chee where an old man took pity on me.

He wanted to know why I wore only a singlet and short pants. I had removed my uniform as it was a sure giveaway. I knew that there would be locals who were Japanese spies and that they would report my whereabouts. I took a chance and asked the old man for help.

He was quite nice and he could speak English. He said he would help, but he could not give me shelter because the Japanese had already made a record of how many people stayed in his house. If they found an extra person there, everyone in the household would be shot. But he gave me an old coat and a pair of pants that he didn't want. He also gave me $2.

He made it clear I had to move on.

With this change of clothes, I started for Katong, where my elder brother lived. But it was very difficult. There were military police everywhere and they had their spies too. At one point, the Japanese stopped me and asked me where I was from. I said I was from Singapore and that I worked here.

"What kind of work do you do?" the Japanese officer asked through an interpreter.

"I sell ice cream," I lied.

They laughed and told me to go.

The difference between life and death was a simple nod from the local spies. They would stare hard at you while they assessed you under Japanese guard. If the spy nodded, it meant, okay, you could go. If he said something like, "Umph!" that was it. You went to the other side to join the gangsters they were rounding up. That was the end of you.

I guess I was lucky they believed my story. I was given a pass in the form of a piece of cloth.

At Frankel Estate, another old man who lived with his wife, came to my aid. He was of Baba descent too and I guess that may have motivated him to help. At that time, of course, the place was just made up of a row of attap houses.

He took a chance on me. He told me, "You can stay at our house from eight or nine o'clock at night, but during the day, you have to leave. The Japanese always come around in the daytime. You can only stay here during the night."

One night as I limped into the old man's house, I saw a third party there, a woman. She asked me why I was limping. I dared not tell her because I didn't know if she was a spy or not, but the old man said, "Don't be afraid. You can tell her."

I told her the whole story. She examined my leg and told me to wait while she went back to her house. It turned out she was a nurse. She returned with some instruments and pulled out the bullet from my leg. She then applied medicine on the wound. She probably saved my leg.

The next morning, I tried to find a way out to Katong. But all the roads were barricaded and even the piece of cloth that I showed the sentries seemed of no use. They barked at me, "*Kurrah!*"

For three days I tried in vain to get past them until one Malay middle-aged man took pity on me and asked, "Baba, Baba, where do you want to go?"

"I want to go to Katong. I've been trying for so many days, but I can't get past the guards," I told him.

He said, "Follow me," and took me through a route off the beaten track. We managed to reach Geylang Serai where there were no military police. From there, I managed to find my way to Katong.

I went straight to my brother's house. He was so happy to see me because he had been worried sick about my safety. But he too could not give me shelter as it would have jeopardised the safety of his whole family. He gave me $10 and told me to get a haircut and make my way back to Malacca.

I got myself a haircut and headed for town, looking for a bus to Malacca. There were no services. The whole city was in chaos. The only way out was by train to the nearest town to Malacca, so I walked from Katong to the Railway Station.

At the Railway Station, the Japanese were still at it. Screening and more screening. My life hung in the balance once again.

I was lucky. I got through.

I made it back to Malacca and hid in the attic of my house for three months as the Japanese had made a record of how many people lived in my house. I went through hell, really. And during that period I lost my sanity at the thought that I had been so close to losing my life.

Secret germ warfare laboratory

People were definitely used as guinea pigs for biological warfare experiments in Singapore during World War Two, said an American historian who has done extensive research on the area, Dr Sheldon Harris.

He also revealed that the Japanese had such biological warfare laboratories not only in Singapore, but also in Rangoon and Manila.

In September 1991, The Straits Times exposed details of a biological warfare laboratory that existed in Singapore during the Japanese Occupation.

The existence of the laboratory was secret and the local people who worked there believed that the experiments were aimed at prevention of epidemics. Little did they know that the reverse was the case.

Dr Harris said "the key evidence" that indicated human beings were used as guinea pigs in Singapore was the arrival on the island at the time of one particular senior Japanese officer, Ryoichi Naito, who brought in 1,000 members of the Southern Army to work in the laboratory.

Naito was a close aide to Japan's most notorious biological warfare expert, Major Shiro Ishii, whom Dr Harris described as "the person most responsible for converting Manchuria into a huge biological warfare laboratory during the Japanese Occupation".

He said firmly, "If Naito was in Singapore, there is no doubt in my mind that there was human experimentation."

Dr Harris is a Professor of History at California State University. He has been researching since 1984 into the Japanese efforts at biological warfare during World War Two.

He said that while the Japanese are commonly believed to have caused 3,000 civilian deaths with their germ warfare experiments, mainly in Manchuria, "my figures reveal that the minimum number tested would be 10,000 people in mainland China, that is China and the northeastern provinces that we call Manchuria".

In Nanking, China, Ishii's men gave youngsters chocolates filled with anthrax germs. "The children were expected to contract the disease and cause an epidemic, which they did. Ishii also distributed dumplings injected with either typhoid or paratyphoid germs to 3,000 Chinese POWs and sent them home to spread the disease," said Dr Harris.

"The Japanese established similar labs in Singapore, Manila and Rangoon to study tropical diseases like malaria to complement research into cold climate diseases in Manchuria," he added.

Dr Harris said, "Virtually every one of the labs involved with biological warfare were conducting human experiments. I have confirmed that there were 18 such labs in China, especially in Harbin, Canton and Mukden, where human experiments took place on a massive scale. I see no reason why Singapore would have been an exception, given the pattern of Japanese experimentation."

Ishii began his secret testing of germ warfare in Harbin after he was posted there on August 31, 1932. His Togo Unit later became known as Unit 731 and was the leader in its field, although there were other units independent of Ishii's authority, but working closely with his forces. The Singapore laboratory is believed to have been a branch of Ishii's Unit 731.

"Ishii enjoyed boasting to his friends that Japan's biological warfare project was his 'secret of secrets'," said Dr Harris.

In the following pages, Mr Othman Wok, the former Minister for Social Affairs, explodes those secrets with details of the Singapore laboratory, where he was employed as a laboratory assistant, competely unaware of the true nature of his work.

Mr Othman was lucky to get out of the laboratory alive, said Dr Harris. He explained, "The Japanese covered up the evidence of their labs very carefully. All the labs were destroyed and prisoners and people marked for experiments were killed. The only survivors were those at the very low levels who did manual work."

Dr Harris classified Mr Othman's designation as manual, the lowest level in the hierarchy, adding, "which is why he had no knowledge of the experiments".

The Japanese government has denied the existence of any such laboratory in Singapore, saying, "According to records in the possession of the Government, there is no mention of any branches of the (731) Unit outside mainland China."

After the war, neither Ishii nor any of his men under United States control were ever prosecuted for war crimes. Instead, it is believed that the Americans co-opted the Japanese biological warfare experts into their own covert programmes.

One returned American POW, Frank James, a victim of germ warfare experiments in Mukden, said, "After the war, the US Army made us sign a statement saying that we would not tell what happened to us in the prison camp before any audiences or newspapers, under threat of court-martial."

Several members of Unit 731 later rose to influential positions in Japan, becoming university professors, deans of medical schools and heads of leading universities and institutes.

Meeting Othman Wok

The Malays did not give the kind of support to the Japanese that some people think, reveals the former Minister for Social Affairs. His own experiences give an insight into life for the Malay community, which was economically depressed during pre-war times and was misled by propaganda about lower prices and a better life under Japanese rule.

His other major revelation is a fascinating first-hand account of a secret biological warfare laboratory in which Mr Othman unwittingly served as a lab assistant for more than two years from mid-1942.

After the war, Mr Othman worked for the Malay newspaper Utusan Melayu as a reporter, rising through the ranks to become Deputy Editor. He left the newspaper in 1963 to go into full-time politics as a member of the ruling People's Action Party. He was appointed Minister for Social Affairs, a post he held from 1963 to 1977 before he became the ambassador to Indonesia. He left his diplomatic post in 1980.

Mr Othman continues to lead an active life. He sits on the board of a few companies and he also recently authored a book of ghost stories, which was a bestseller at the 1991 Singapore Bookfair.

Working with death

When I was a little boy, there were many Japanese traders in Singapore, concentrated in Middle Road and High Street. This was way before the war. I had an uncle who worked for one of their toy shops in High Street and I recall him taking me there when I was five years old. His Japanese boss gave me toys to take home.

They also sold rubber shoes, shirts and all sorts of knickknacks for very low prices. A pair of rubber shoes was priced at only twenty cents. You could get most things in those shops for ten cents, which is how they came to be called ten-cent stalls.

There were also Japanese fishermen in Siglap, living side by side with the Malays. During the night, they went around the kampung hawking Japanese cakes on a push-cart. When I was a boy of ten, I used to play in the village with the Japanese children. Their community was fluent in Malay and they were very friendly people. What we didn't know then was that many of these Japanese, be they storekeepers, photographers or fishermen, were spies for the Japanese government.

When they saw a rift develop between the different Muslim groups, they seized the opportunity and cleverly exploited it to their advantage. You see, the only Malay newspaper at that time, the Warta Malaya, was controlled by the Arabs, who were businessmen. The Malays were unhappy because the newspaper voiced only the Arab community's concerns and aspirations. So the Malays started their own newspaper in 1939, called Utusan Melayu.

When the Utusan Melayu was born, a war of words ensued between the different Muslim groups. And the British liked it. It suited their style of "divide and rule", you see. Well, they didn't encourage it, but they didn't take any action against it either. They liked the idea of the Malays, Arabs and the Indian-Muslims at loggerheads with each other.

The Japanese approached some of the editors of Utusan Melayu to print their propaganda. The editors agreed and the Malays were fed with propaganda that if the Japanese took over Singapore, the price of rice would drop. They claimed that a *kati* of rice that cost eight cents would be sold for only two cents under Japanese rule. And the Malays began believing that Singapore would be much better under the Japanese than under the British — because of the propaganda that was printed. Of course, the British took action and jailed some of the editors.

When the first bombs fell, it was about four o'clock in the morning and I was sound asleep.

At that time we were staying in the school quarters of the Tanjong Katong Malay School at Wilkinson Road, where my father taught. It was near the Paya Lebar airport where the British had their fighter planes, the famous Brewster Buffaloes. They were reputed to be the best in the world. But, as you know, they got knocked down by the Zeros like flies during the war. Anyway in that first spate of bombing, the impact of the explosions caused the quarters to shake and the windows of my room to rattle. That startled me out of bed. In fact, the whole family was awakened and pandemonium followed as we tried to figure out what was happening.

Then we heard the siren — after the first bombs had fallen.

We had been told in the newspapers and over the radio that when you heard the siren, you were to take shelter. But we had no air-raid shelter. All the talk of war had fallen on deaf ears as we went about our business smug in the knowledge that the British were invincible. And now here we were, sitting ducks for the Japanese. The whole of Singapore was ablaze with lights that early morning when the Japanese attacked. So much for a defence.

Luckily, however, our quarters was on stilts, so we scrambled under the house onto the cold, cemented ground.

The raid did not last very long. With the exception of some British aeroplanes taking off in a delayed reaction, we heard nothing more. After about half-an-hour on that cold floor, we decided it was safe to go back into the house. But we still didn't go back to sleep.

Later that day, I had to sit for my History paper as the Cambridge exams were on. I remember it was History because I was quite worried about that paper; it wasn't my strongest subject. My father said I should go for the exam. "This is your last year," he reminded me.

I remember clearly the bus ride to school. People were in a panic. The whole of Singapore city was on the move. Lorries were loaded and people moved this way and that without any sense of purpose. You could feel the tension in the air.

For the first time in my life, I bought an English newspaper, the Malaya Tribune, for five cents, and read about the Japanese landing in Kota Baru.

I reached Raffles Institution at about eight o'clock that morning and the look on the faces of the British volunteer soldiers who had occupied the school building said it all. They were bewildered.

There was no air raid that day, but the planes did come back during the exams, making us run for shelter in the school compound, where there were trenches dug by the soldiers. Some students had to hide inside the school toilets because the trenches couldn't accommodate all of us. And although the teachers tried their utmost to stick to exam rules, it was impossible to restrain us from exchanging notes on the exam questions as we waited out the Japanese bombing!

When the bombing intensified, my family moved from Wilkinson Road to Jalan Eunos to put up with a friend's family. We figured it was wise not to live near the airport, which was a prime target of the Japanese.

I was only seventeen at the time and thought the war was exciting. When there was a siren, I'd rush out together with my friend to catch a glimpse of the planes even though, for the most part, we couldn't see them because they were hidden by the clouds.

It was only after the exams that the horror of war was brought home to me. It happened on the day that my friend and I responded to advertisements in the newspapers for bank clerks at Chartered Bank (there was a shortage of staff because some people just stopped going to work). We were on our way to the bank at Battery Road for an interview when we were caught by an air raid and had to take refuge near Empress Place. After the raid, my friend said we'd better go home so we abandoned our plans and headed home.

But when we got back to Jalan Eunos, we found the area had been bombed. Somebody must have tipped off the Japanese that there was a headquarters for volunteer soldiers in the area. The bomb had missed its target and landed on our village, wiping out a house and cutting the occupants to pieces.

Only then did the fear hit me, you know, because before that we hadn't seen anyone injured or killed by the bombs. Up till then it had just been an exciting adventure. But now this... the whole kampung turned upside down. And the dead... arms and legs chopped off, lay among the ruins for us to gape at in horror. I realised then that this was a real war. And those victims could have been us.

Right up to this point, we had been quite happy to make do without a bomb shelter, but now the kampung menfolk got together to build one on the side of the hill on which the kampung stood. We dug a trench and covered it with coconut trunks.

It was a solid shelter, but we never got to use it.

By the time we had completed the shelter, it was February 13, and the Japanese forces poured through Tampines right down to our village at Jalan Eunos. They were a frightening sight. The expression on their faces was so fierce that we barricaded ourselves in our houses.

The soldiers knocked on our doors and told us to flee the village because they expected a counterattack from the British. We followed their orders and retreated to Kampung Kembangan.

Sure enough, the British later fired from Pulau Blakang Mati and from Fort Canning. They also sent up their armoured trucks. There was a massive battle just in front of my friend's house, and we were to later learn that the Japanese used the shelter we had laboriously built to their advantage.

The battle lasted all night. We could hear the tumultuous progress from where we were at Kampung Kembangan.

The following evening, we hesitantly made our way back to find everything very quiet. We saw dead bodies strewn all over the place. The casualties were largely on the side of the British: the Indian crew of the armoured vehicles lay dead on the road.

Some of the kampung houses were razed to the ground. Yet the shelter we had built, although bullet-ridden, was otherwise undamaged and there were no bodies inside. The Japanese troops who used it must have survived.

The next morning, February 15, we heard that the British had surrendered.

On the sixteenth, we moved back to our Wilkinson quarters, using a small lorry to ferry our belongings. There were many road blocks manned by Japanese sentries and it was difficult to get past them. We didn't know their lingo and they didn't know ours. But news had spread by word of mouth that the Malays should put on their *songkoks* (Malay headdress). When the Japanese saw us wearing *songkoks*, they let us pass, and the Malay population sighed with relief. The Japanese also released the Malay newspaper editors whom the British had jailed as collaborators.

But the chaos persisted. Looting was rampant. The first wave of Japanese joined in the looting too. They also raped women. They took away the daughter of a neighbour and raped her for a week. When she returned, she could hardly walk. The Chinese were their main target, so they seldom went to a Malay house, unless they were very drunk. But some Malay girls fell victim too.

We were worried about the safety of my sister who was sixteen years old at that time. Whenever the Japanese passed by our house, we locked her in the toilet. We also told her not to comb her hair, hoping that it would put them off.

Fortunately, my uncle who had worked in the Japanese High Street store was living with us. He managed to get some posters from the Japanese police explaining that he had worked for the Japanese before. We plastered these on our front door. When the soldiers came around and saw these posters, we were spared the indignities that many others suffered.

Also, our living quarters was in a school compound with a fence surrounding it. There was a gate that led to the quarters that we kept locked at all times. So, in a sense we were quite safe. I emphasise "quite" because we did get the occasional stray soldier who wandered into our compound, drunk. We had to talk nicely to them and pacify them. My uncle's smattering knowledge of Japanese was put to good use here.

Another helpful thing was that the Japanese air force staff took over the vacant houses in the area, presumably because they were near the airport. The pilots were better educated than the average infantry soldiers, so we could move relatively freely within the boundaries they occupied — Mountbatten, Katong and Geylang roads — with a pass that they issued us.

Others had it bad. In different parts of Singapore, the Chinese were hauled from their homes and asked to squat on a field for three days and three nights without water. I saw thousands of Chinese squatting on a small field at the corner of Telok Kurau Road and Changi Road under Japanese guard. Some of them were my schoolmates from Raffles Institution.

Once as I passed that field, I saw someone I knew well. I wanted to speak to him, but the Japanese guard shooed me away. But on another occasion, the guard was far away and this friend of mine called to me and said,

"Please, can you bring me water? I've been here for two days. Look at my brothers."

He pointed to the dehydrated, petrified children. They urinated there, they shat there, they did everything there. It was a wretched sight. I pitied him and so on my next trip past the field, I brought a bottle of water that I stashed away in a small gunny bag that I used as a carry bag. I threw the bottle in his direction as I passed. I don't know whether he got it or not because I walked away quickly, not daring to stop as the sentries, with bayonets fixed, were making their rounds.

Later I learnt that many of these Chinese were singled out and shot. We heard machine-gun fire at the Lucky Heights area continuously. That area was covered with jungle then and I didn't know what the gunfire was all about. But people later said that was where the Japanese massacred the Chinese and people who were pro-British, like the Indians and the Eurasians. They were asked to dig their own graves.

As for me, when I saw the way the Japanese were slapping and shoving people around, I made up my mind that I would have nothing to do with them. But I still needed to make a living to survive, so I went to my granduncle, a fisherman in Siglap village, and told him, "I don't want to work with the Japanese, I want to be a fisherman."

"All right, you can work with me," he said.

I spent my nights on the kelong from then on. I came back to the mainland only in the mornings.

Once in a while, my father bought some fish and asked me to sell it. I rode from village to village on my bicycle, going from door to door selling the fish. Business was not bad, especially as people were scared to go to the market. My work as a fishmonger helped us get by.

One day, however, I was spotted by a squad of six or seven Japanese soldiers who were patrolling the village on bicycle.

"*Sakana*!" they said — *sakana* means fish in Japanese — and they took away the fish without paying. Who dared to protest against those fellas? They were a fierce and ruthless lot. I watched helplessly as they rode away with my entire day's earnings.

A month later, the same thing happened, but this time it was a different patrol squad in Changi. They made off with all the fish without paying a cent. After the second incident, my father came to the decision that I should give up my job as a fishmonger. These unfortunate occurrences had eaten into our capital and we were losing money. So my fish selling days came to an abrupt halt.

It was around then that the Japanese formed the Singapore Malay Union to encourage the Malays to join the military. The *Heiho*, it was called. It was a force made up of local chaps purportedly to defend Singapore. My father was very worried that I would be recruited into the *Heiho*. So he begged me to go to school instead.

At that time, the only schools open were those that taught Japanese. I was reluctant to learn their language, but my father warned, "They are looking for young people like you to recruit into the *Heiho*. And there are rumours that they will send the *Heiho* to Indonesia and other places to fight the Allied forces."

So I took his advice and enrolled in a Japanese school at Oxley Rise. I spent the next three to four months learning Japanese, from *Katakana* right up to the tricky *Hiragana* script.

In the evenings, I tried to make some money on the black market. People would say, "I have this very nice Australian lipstick, you know. Can you get someone to buy it?"

At that time, the Japanese encouraged people to gamble, so New World, Happy World and Great World were full of gamblers. And those places had hostesses who needed make-up, so I sent my "kakis" out to make the sale.

But the most frequent sales I made involved cigarettes. You see, we were all given a cigarette ration and since I didn't smoke, it was an item I could trade for something I really needed. So I queued up patiently at the designated shops to get my ration of cigarettes, which I then took to Kandang Kerbau and sold. That was the place where everybody congregated for black market activities, the old Tekhar market. You went to the backlane and cut your deals there with other people much like yourself.

In late 1942, my uncle, the one who knew Japanese, told me there was a vacancy in the Anti-plague Laboratory, where he worked. It was situated in a military complex called the *Okai 9420 Butai*. My uncle set up an interview and told me to bargain for a high salary. He said, "Don't go below $1.50 a day."

I saw the colonel in charge of the Personnel Department, who knew a smattering of English. He sent me to work straight away to try me out. After three days, they were satisfied with my work, so I was sent down to see him again, this time to fix my salary.

He said, "How much do you want?"

I said, "$1.50."

"$1.50? Too high!"

"But this work is quite dangerous because we're dealing with rats," I replied hesitantly. My uncle had said I was to bargain, but it was my first job and I didn't know how far to push.

"No, no, no," he said. "You got uniform. Not dangerous. $1.20."

We did indeed have white overalls, rubber boots, rubber gloves and a headdress. And I wanted the job badly because of the rice ration. I thought, what's thirty cents? Although at that time, it was big money. You could buy six plates of mee goreng for five cents each! Anyway, I said, "Okay, $1.20 a day."

That was what I was paid, $1.20 a day, $36 a month.

I worked as a lab assistant, together with two other Malays, three Chinese and two Indian boys. Our job was to pick fleas from the rats which were brought in by another department — the rat collectors — and breed them in a clean, empty kerosene tank, in which there was a bed of sand. Very fine sand, plus some unknown powdered chemical and dried blood, either from a horse or a cow. The blood was prepared by drying it on a tray and grinding it into a fine powder. We mixed it with the sand and the mysterious chemical product that the Japanese soldiers prepared from bottles.

We worked under two colonels and four senior privates. I have no recollection of their names. At that time it was just a job I did for survival. If I knew then that this lab was going to make history, I would have taken down the names of the officers. But who would have guessed at that time?

My uncle was working in the rat collection department. There were about forty or fifty staff there. Every morning, they went out with two or three military trucks all over Singapore to set traps. (Ed: a wire box with a piece of copra inside. People were offered fifty cents for each rat they trapped.)

My lab took fifteen or twenty rats daily, both from the town area and the kampung. The Japanese wanted to study the difference between the rats from the two areas. The town rats were big, but they had very little fur because they lived in the drains. The rats from the kampung areas had very nice, thick fur.

We put the rats in glass cubicles that had a piece of cotton soaked in chloroform. The rats became drowsy, as did the fleas, and this facilitated our job. We picked the fleas with pincers and put them in a glass vessel with water before transferring them to the kerosene container. The Japanese soldiers, supervised by the colonels, injected the rats with a plague serum and left them alone for about two weeks.

Then the fleas that we had bred in the kerosene container were fed the blood of the infected rats. The Japanese picked out about ten fleas a day for that. The process went like this; the infected rats were put in glass containers. Each container had a piece of cotton soaked in chloroform so that after one or two minutes, they became half-conscious. From experience we learnt that it was absolutely essential that the rat was sufficiently drugged because there was one occasion when an infected rat bit through a Japanese private's rubber glove and the accident killed him. An Indian chap who suffered the same accident was rushed to the hospital and had to have the tip of his finger cut off.

Anyway, each drugged rat was then laid on a board and its legs tied to four poles. A patch of fur on its belly was shaved off. Then the ten fleas they picked from our breeding can were allowed to get their fill of the rat's blood. This was done by tipping a test tube with the fleas over the rat's shaven belly. When the fleas stopped jumping about, the Japanese knew that they had taken in as much blood as they could so they returned the bloated fleas to the breeding can. Subsequently, of course, all the fleas in the breeding can were infected.

Once a month, the soldiers put all the fleas that were infected in big glass bottles and took them by lorry to the Tanjong Pagar Railway Station under heavy escort. We learnt from one of the local Malay drivers, who understood Japanese and overheard the soldiers speaking, that the fleas were to be taken to Thailand.

That was the sum total of our knowledge of those experiments. You see, nobody dared ask questions. Who dared ask? If you asked questions, the Japanese would probably have said, "Why do you want to know so much?"

I mean, they were the masters, you know, and they were not guys you could joke with, much less ask questions that didn't concern you. They were always serious. A joke could even get you beaten up. I had a friend who joked with the Japanese and was beaten up because they didn't find him funny. But they were military people in those days. Not like the Japanese that you see now, who are very nice people.

Although the sign on my workplace said, "Anti-plague Laboratory," I never suspected that I worked in a germ warfare laboratory until I read in The Straits Times in September 1945 that the Japanese bombed Chongqing with bottles of fleas.

Anyway, I left my job at the lab in mid-1944 and went to work in the Harbour Board as a clerk in the water department because they offered me a bigger rice ration. At the lab, I got eight *katies* a month, whereas at the Harbour Board, I got twelve. In those days, the salary did not count as much as the rice ration.

Leaving the lab job was easy; I just walked off. There was no such thing as giving notice at that time.

There was no real system, everything was topsy-turvy.

My boss at the Harbour Board was a Japanese, but he could speak Malay. He was quite a nice man and I remember him well; his name was Sakara-san.

Our job was to supply all the ships that were docked in the harbour with fresh water from the water hydrants 500 to 1,000 metres from the wharves.

While I was at the Harbour Board, I met many POWs because they worked as labourers, unloading cargo from the ships. They were very skinny, and always hungry. They always asked us for cigarettes, which I gave them on the quiet. They actively bartered with the local population.

On one occasion, one of them pointed to his belt and whispered to me, "I have this really nice leather belt that I'll trade for some cakes."

I left the dockside secretly and bought some cakes, exchanging them for the belt. It was a dangerous thing to do, of course. If the POWs were caught receiving food from us they would have been beaten severely and I would have got it too.

During their lunch hour, the POWs mixed the rice ration that they received with palm oil that dripped out of a tank. The oil was very dirty and not for consumption. It was stored for fuel.

When I asked them, "Why do you do it?" they explained that the oil made it easier for them to go to the toilet. Otherwise, as they were given only cold water and rice, they often suffered from constipation.

They couldn't understand the Japanese guards, and were slapped about all the time. Although they were our masters at one time, I felt sorry for them. Once a proud people, now being treated like animals by the Japanese.

I think if the British were in the same position, they would not have treated the Japanese like that, because they were sticklers for conventions. But the Japanese didn't go by that. They beat up the POWs with poles, their rifles, whatever they could get a hold of.

The POWs were not the only ones who were abused by the Japanese. When I worked at the harbour, I often saw shiploads of Indonesians arriving; men in black and beautiful Indonesian girls in white uniforms.

The Indonesian women said, "We are going to be nurses!" What they really ended up being was comfort girls for the Japanese. They were literally kept prisoner in a row of houses at Katong Road.

After the war, many of these girls escaped to a Malay kampung in Amber Road with the help of the young men of that village. Disgraced, they did not want to go back to Indonesia, and many married the locals.

When I asked the Indonesian men the purpose of their visit, they replied enthusiastically, "Oh, the Japanese have promised that if we follow them to Thailand, we will have a better life."

Some of them were sixty to seventy years old. They were sent to toil on the Death Railway in Thailand, but many others never made it that far because the Allies' intense bombing at that period made the journey up there impossible.

So, many of them were stuck in Singapore with no place to stay. They became beggars. Towards the end of the war, you could find them dying like flies from hunger and malnutrition on the roadside. No one cared because there was a hell of a lot of confusion towards the end of the war and the Japanese simply could not provide for them.

When the surrender was announced, there was a period from '45 till the end of the year when many of the Indonesians who had gone to the Death Railway returned to Singapore. They hoped to go back to Indonesia from here. But there were no ships. So when they arrived, they too became beggars. They went around to the refuse bins looking for food. They led a wretched life. Hundreds of them died on the roadside.

In comparison, I count my blessings that I had my family network to depend on and my father was an enterprising man. He had contacts on the Indonesian Riau islands. There was plenty of food there because they had land to plant rice. But they were in need of cloth. It was a difficult commodity to get. I recall how my trousers were so thick with patching and repatching that they took a good three days to dry.

But we did manage to get cloth — our old blankets and clothes — and in return the Indonesians, who came to Singapore by sampan, gave us precious rice, dried fish, vegetables and chickens. I recall selling one of the melons they brought in for two hundred Japanese dollars! But the currency had inflated to such a ridiculous extent by then that it only got me a bit of rice on the black market.

I had a bicycle so it was easier to move around and cut deals with people who wanted the goods we had. But when I came across the soldiers, I had to bow and if I didn't, I got slapped. I was slapped around quite a few times, maybe because I bowed wrongly or maybe because the soldiers just wanted to be nasty for no rhyme or reason. Some of these Japanese, on a whim, would beckon you to come to them, look around, slap you and walk off. No explanations given. Very peculiar people.

But they were the masters.

Although the newspapers trumpeted one Japanese victory after another and reported their enemies annihilated, I wasn't caught by surprise like most of the population when the Japanese surrendered because my family had a clandestine radio.

I was at the harbour when the British destroyer arrived to regain control of Singapore. The first thing the British captain asked my Malay boss when he landed was where the Japanese were. He was told that the Japanese Harbour Board officials were in an office building nearby. On his instructions, my boss called them to the dock where they were told to line up in a row.

Then the captain said, "Tell the Japanese to go to the internment camp in Jurong. And they should walk there. Tell them not to try and escape. If they try to escape, they will be shot."

So my boss translated this to the Japanese. I helped too, since I was familiar with the language. The Japanese officials said, "Okay, okay."

Then they bowed to us.

It was the first time the Japanese bowed to us. We felt great. Events had turned one full cycle.

A businessman's lot

Business was good during the Occupation — if you were a black marketeer.

However, there were other opportunities and two out of the next three people tell what it was like to be a businessman under the Japanese Occupation.

Mr Tan Keong Choon was one businessman who had to run for his life because he was the nephew of a major anti-Japanese figure, Tan Kah Kee. His story reveals what it was like for someone whose business collapsed with the arrival of the Japanese.

Mr Lim Bo Yam, the brother of another famous anti-Japanese figure, Lim Bo Seng, had better luck. The Japanese wanted him to continue running the family brickworks factory, so he survived.

During the Occupation, Mr Mohammad Ghazali Caffoor was much younger than the other two businessmen, but displayed keen commercial instincts even as a boy. He also tells what it was like for his father who ran a restaurant under Japanese licence.

When the Japanese came, I dropped everything and walked out of my office. It was like leaving a house on fire.

— Honorary President of Singapore Chinese Chamber of Commerce Tan Keong Choon.

Japanese soldiers at Raffles Square

Meeting Tan Keong Choon

The arrival of the Japanese sent many people into hiding. Among their number was the nephew of Tan Kah Kee, the leader of the anti-Japanese movement. Mr Tan Keong Choon was twenty-three years old at the time and had started his own import-export business just the year before.

"When the Japanese came, I just dropped everything and walked out of my shop. It was like leaving a house on fire. What can you save?"

Indeed, he had every reason to act with urgency. There was a price on his head. The Japanese, alerted by their informers, went after every relative of Tan Kah Kee, who was the leader of the resistance against the Japanese. The Japanese attempted to find and torture any relations of Tan Kah Kee for information on his whereabouts.

But although Mr Tan Keong Choon left in a hurry, he managed to salvage rolls of his canvas stock from a godown. This he sold in exchange for gold bars and diamonds. Then, he and his mother sneaked off to the small villages around Paya Lebar and Changi and hid there until they could make their escape from Singapore.

Mr Tan, an only child, recalls how the Japanese came to the Paya Lebar village looking for young women. "We heard the girls crying and struggling. This went on for several nights. I was thankful that I did not have any sisters."

Later, Mr Tan organised a daring escape with his mother on false identification papers. They fled to Penang by train, eventually making their way to Saigon where they spent the rest of the war years. When Mr Tan returned to Singapore with his mother, he went back into business.

When I met him at his office, Mr Tan was dressed in a coat and tie, which complemented his well-built frame. The first thing that struck me was his height and stature. He has a very distinguished look, his glasses sitting well on a scholarly face, which does not reveal his age. He was born in 1918.

Today, at seventy-three, he manages three different companies, dealing in commodities and property, and holds directorships in several large firms.

He was the President of the Singapore Chinese Chamber of Commerce for two terms from 1973 to 1977, and again in 1983 to 1987. He remains the Honorary President of the Chamber.

His wife is Japanese. Her father went to jail for questioning the war effort in Japan. Mr Tan met her after the war and they married in 1948. They have one son.

His life and exploits have had a very revealing effect on Mr Tan. He exudes self-confidence. You can see that he is a self-made man. Although he had to write off his business because of the war, it did not stop him from starting "all over again, right from the bottom".

One other thing that struck me was his strong concern that I should present the facts regarding the war accurately and not portray the period through rose-tinted glasses.

What follows is his story in his own words...

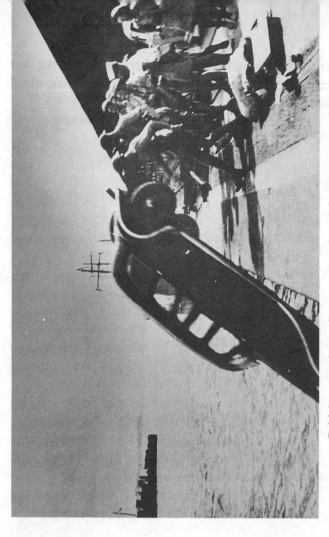

I expect every scrap of material to be blown to pieces to prevent capture by the enemy.

— British Prime Minister Winston Churchill's instructions on January 20, 1942, on the defence of Singapore.

British troops destroying property when defeat seemed imminent

A price on his head

I was a year old when my parents brought me to Singapore. My father, Tan Kah Kee's younger brother, was to take over the family business here while Tan Kah Kee returned to China to oversee the development of a school and university in Amoy that they had established. But soon after, around 1921, I returned to China with my parents as my father had developed tuberculosis. I studied in Amoy right up to 1937.

I returned to Singapore that year for the summer holidays to meet my relatives. I was supposed to be here for only a short stay, but even as I made my way to Singapore, the Sino-Japanese war broke out and I was forced to stay put in Singapore right up to 1939.

Subsequently, I returned to China and completed my education at Chinan University in Shanghai. I could not return to Amoy as there was too much fear and confusion there because the Japanese were in Occupation.

In 1940, I formed a trading company in Shanghai with my base in Singapore, which I thought was more secure. It was the Impregnable Fortress of the British.

My business here was based at a small shop at No. 78, North Canal Road. The shophouse really belonged to my uncle, Tan Kah Kee. He sold biscuits downstairs and I had a modest office upstairs, which I shared with his second son. It is still there, although the facade has changed and it belongs to someone else now.

I put my life savings of $3,000 into that business. I was a young man then just starting out, trying to make a living. I conducted an import-export business in such things as tea, textiles and talcum powder.

When the first bombs fell on Singapore in 1941, I was sound asleep in rented premises in Geylang where I lived with my mother. It was only the next morning, when she woke me up and told me, "The bombs have been dropped, you know," that I realised war had come to Singapore. We anxiously studied the developments of the war.

By January 1942, the Japanese had overrun most of Malaya and there did not seem much hope that the British could hold out. They were retreating faster than the Japanese were attacking.

I went to see Tan Kah Kee sometime around the end of the month and advised him to run away. I told him there was no point in him staying in Singapore because the British could not protect him.

But my uncle told me, "The British will not allow me to leave Singapore."

They needed him to recruit labourers for the dockyards, organise street patrols to maintain order and spread the British propaganda to the Chinese population.

My uncle did a remarkable job in meeting the British demands. But he was a very distressed man at that time. He had suffered staggering losses as his stocks of rubber in Ipoh, worth more than a million dollars, had fallen into the hands of the Japanese. On top of that, he had to assume the leadership of the Singapore Chinese Mobilisation Council, formed to help the British defend Singapore.

Certain factions in the Chinese community insisted that the Chinese be armed to defend Singapore. My uncle was dead set against this, although he knew the British would jump at the idea. It would serve them well because once the Chinese took up arms against the Japanese, there would surely be no cooperation between the two racial groups if the Japanese conquered Singapore.

Tan Kah Kee knew that for the Chinese it would mean political suicide to take up arms now, especially if the Japanese overran Singapore. Besides, as my uncle pointed out, if the British needed reinforcements, they could get them from Australia and India within a month. He also stressed that the Chinese would need at least six months' training to be able to make a positive contribution to the defence of the island.

Unfortunately, supporters of Ng Yeh-lu, the communist leader, overrode his wishes for their own political motivations. Poorly armed Chinese then took up positions against the Japanese barely five days before the invading force attacked the island. History proved my uncle correct and there were severe reprisals against the Chinese community because of their armed defence.

The British promised my uncle a berth on a ship or aircraft should things take a turn for the worse. "Oh, don't worry," they told him.

But in the end, when the British requisitioned all the motor launches for their own use, my uncle had to secretly escape to Sumatra on a friend's motorboat on February 3, together with a group of other Chinese leaders wanted by the Japanese. He did not even have time to say goodbye to the family. Fortunately, they too managed to escape.

When the British surrendered Singapore, I dropped everything and walked out of my office. It was just like leaving a house on fire. What could you save? There was a price on my head because Tan Kah Kee was my uncle, so escape was my main objective.

I went to the OCBC godown, where some of my business stocks were kept. I wanted to sell them to obtain money for my escape. Unfortunately, my stocks of tea which were way inside the godown had been stolen. Luckily though, some canvas that I had imported for the purpose of covering vehicles was untouched, although it was in the front portion of the godown. That lot of canvas saved my life.

I had purchased the canvas for $10,000, but I managed to sell it for $100,000. Such goods commanded a premium when the Japanese came in and the country's economy and resources depleted rapidly. With that money, I purchased gold and diamonds.

My mother and I then went into hiding in an obscure kampung in a rubber estate around Paya Lebar to bide our time. I had a distant relative who lived there, Tan Lark

Sye, the father of Nanyang University. He provided us with an attap house, which we shared with some of my mother's relatives.

The Japanese came to the village looking for women they could rape. This went on for several nights. We saw the soldiers going into a rich man's bungalow next door because he had many daughters. We heard the girls crying and struggling. I was thankful that I did not have any sisters.

Later, the Japanese received a tip-off that Yeh-lu was hiding in the village where my mother and I lived. They organised a door to door manhunt for him.

I had a very close shave then. Just as I was about to step out of the hut to make a run for it, a soldier walked in. For some strange reason, he did not stop me. I did not hesitate for a moment. I headed straight for a village in Changi. I did not dare take the risk of walking on the main road as I was aware that the Japanese had set up barricades. I made my way there through the cover of rubber estates and jungles.

At that time, much of Changi and Paya Lebar was undeveloped, which was why we had opted to move there in the first place. The journey to Changi was rough but I managed it somehow. I had to leave my mother behind with my relatives at Paya Lebar. She must have been worried sick for my safety.

I stayed with a friend who was related to Chinese officials who supported the Japanese puppet government in China. I was safe in his house so I stayed for about six

195

to seven months.

When things quietened down, I went to the Beach Road police station to apply for travel documents to Penang for my mother and me under false identities. I called myself Tan Hock Guan. It was a big risk I took, but they didn't ask any questions, and I got the documents.

With the gold and diamonds I had purchased, we bought our way out of the country. We went to Penang first and stayed with a relative there. Then we went up to Bangkok and eventually made it to Saigon, where we stayed until the end of the war.

After the war, we went back to China. Shanghai was in bad shape and my business was in shambles. I had to start all over again, right from the bottom.

War is brutal and ugly. You can't possibly know what it is like unless you experience it yourself. As the Buddhists say, "You have to drink the water to know whether it is warm, hot, or cold." You have to drink it yourself and only then will you know.

Yet, the war years did prove that we are a very resilient people. Whatever the pressures, if you have the iron will to survive, you will. If you can't, you might as well bury yourself.

Meeting Lim Bo Yam

Mr Lim Bo Yam, born in 1911, is the younger brother of Lim Bo Seng, the anti-Japanese activist who is celebrated in the annals of Singapore as a war hero. In the living room of his elegant family home in the exclusive Shelford Road area, hangs a life-sized portrait of their pioneering industrialist father, Lim Chee Gee. The Japanese soldiers bayonetted the painting, but it has since been restored to its former glory. It was painted by the famous Chinese artist, Peon Nu, for the princely sum of $2,700 way back in 1927. (Apparently, Peon Nu also did a painting of Governor Sir Shenton Thomas.)

When Lim Bo Seng fled Singapore shortly before the Japanese arrived, he placed the family business in Lim Bo Yam's hands. The younger Mr Lim is a very reserved man with gracious manners. He spoke with a distinct Hongkong accent and showed a great deal of attachment to China, where he has several relatives. He has six daughters, three of them live in Australia, another in Honolulu, and his only son lives in New Zealand.

Mr Lim spoke with deep regret about the business losses his family suffered during the Japanese Occupation. Nonetheless, there is no denying that his family was better off than average as the Japanese came to rely on their brickworks factories.

It is difficult to fathom the Japanese motives for allowing Mr Lim the relative freedom to run his brick-works business when his elder brother was so high on their wanted list. In the final analysis, one has to conclude that they were just plain desperate.

During the Occupation, however, Mr Lim's life was in constant danger when he resumed contact with his elder brother, who was trained, armed and dangerous — operating in Malaya. However, the Japanese never caught the younger Lim in a compromising position.

Lim Bo Seng was eventually captured in Ipoh in March 1944 and died in prison a few months later. He was thirty-seven years old. Although Mr Lim Bo Yam heard about his brother's death from his sources, he was not allowed to tell his brother's widow. It was a burden of knowledge he had to bear alone.

The mantle of what was left of the family business fell heavily on his shoulders. Shortly after the war, he set up a sawmill factory in Pahang. Since its closure in mid-1970, Mr Lim has been in retirement, keeping busy by dabbling in the stock market.

Bricks that saved his life

My father decided to bring the family to Singapore because there was a civil war in China. Law and order had completely broken down, with bandits often kidnapping children for ransom.

I was fifteen when I came here. My father was already an established businessman here, with factories and a construction firm in his name. The whole of what is now Braddell Heights belonged to him. He owned 147 acres along Braddell Road, stretching from Upper Serangoon Road right down to Lorong Chuan. He set up a massive rubber plantation there because those were the boom years for rubber.

Next to our estate was what is now Toa Payoh. It was just swamp and jungle then. We used to go hunting there for birds and all sorts of animals.

We also owned two of the three brickworks in Singapore at that time. Because my father started as a building contractor, building houses and tendering for government projects, it made sense for him to start a brickworks to supply his own business. In fact, that is how Brickworks District got its name, because we owned a brickworks there. We had another one in Alexandria, directly opposite the ABC Brewery. The third brickworks was at Upper Serangoon at Braddell Road, right at the bottom of Braddell

Heights. It was called the Teng San Brickworks.

Most of our labourers came from China, but we also employed Indians to work in the kilns, which operated under very high temperatures. In fact, we had a Chinese *kepala* (supervisor) and an Indian *kepala*, both responsible for recruiting Chinese and Indian coolies respectively for our brickworks. The Chinese and Indian coolies worked together, but they lived separately.

My brother, Lim Bo Seng, who was two years older than me, managed the whole family business. Before the Japanese came, he was the president of the Chinese Contractor Association. He worked closely with Tan Kah Kee in obtaining money for the China Relief Fund. In fact, our Chinese coolies contributed a monthly sum of about fifty cents or a dollar to the Fund through their *kepala*. It was a substantial portion of their income as labour was cheap then and if memory serves me right, they were paid something like a dollar or two a day.

My brother was very active against the Japanese. When the Sino-Japan war broke out, Bo Seng even went to Dungun in Trengganu where there was a Japanese iron mine to urge the workers to strike.

When the Japanese started bombing Singapore, the dockside labourers refused to work because the bombing was concentrated in their work area. The British became desperate. They promised Bo Seng the world if he could get them labourers.

The Special Branch people said, "You go and get the labourers we require. You help us, and you'll have no need to worry if the Japanese come. If necessary, we'll evacuate your family by submarine."

Wow! That was some promise!

But my brother believed them.

We all thought the British would protect us. The place was crawling with Indian and Australian soldiers. But when Singapore was about to fall, my brother escaped from the island by motorboat through his own efforts. He went from the Riau islands to Sumatra. His last instructions to me were to stay behind and look after the family.

My brother had to escape because like many people involved in the China Relief Fund, he feared he would lose his head if the Japanese caught him. His wife and children fled to St John's Island where she had a doctor friend. There was no help at all from the British. They were busy evacuating their own people.

When the Japanese came in, they started looking for my brother. They got hold of the Chinese and asked them, "Where does Lim Bo Seng stay?"

The locals did not hesitate to tell them where we lived.

Early one morning, about 200 soldiers surrounded our three houses in our Braddell Road estate. It was about six o'clock in the morning when they came knocking.

Boom... boom... boom!

Hoo.. hoo... hooo! (He mimics the way the Japanese spoke.)

They chased everybody out. We could not speak the language so there was no communication with them.

They just kept saying hoo.... hoo... hoo! Signalling us to get out.

They searched the house, presumably for my brother or documents that could lead them to him, but found nothing. In frustration, they put a bayonet through a king-sized painting of my father. The painting was done in 1927 by a renowned artist, Peon Nu, at the cost of $2,700, a fortune in those days.

They marched all the womenfolk to one house and all the menfolk to the compound. In the compound, they tied our hands with wire and attached a helmet between the wires for each person. You see, the British had run away, leaving many steel helmets inside our estate. While this was going on, some of the coolies from the factory came to see what the commotion was all about — and were rounded up too.

The women were locked up in the house and left behind. The males, about twenty-two of us, were marched to a bungalow about one-and-a-half miles away.

There was a fenced-up tennis court in the compound, and the twenty-two of us were put in there. They untied our hands, but put an armed guard over us, so there was no possibility of escape. We were there for two nights, with only biscuits and water for food.

We just sat there, out in the open; nobody actually knew what was happening, or what was going to happen. They told us nothing. We left our lives in the hands of the gods. But the general feeling among us was that we were going to be killed.

After forty-eight hours, some young Japanese military police arrived. They asked us questions through interpreters: "What is your job? Did you take part in any China Relief Fund activities?"

We said everybody in Singapore took part in these activities.

They asked very simple questions, but they looked hard at us. If you were told to step to the right, you got a chop on your shirt, which meant you could travel freely around the island.

Those who were told to step to the left were taken away in a lorry and we never heard from them again. When we reflected on it later, we realised that the one side was heaven and the other, hell.

Out of the twenty-two of us, they took nine away.

Some of us later asked the Japanese interpreters when we saw them in town, "Where have they been taken? So many days, still no news."

"Oh, don't worry, don't worry, they've been taken somewhere to work," the interpreters replied.

Actually, they were shot.

Soon after, the Japanese summoned me because I was in charge of the family business after Bo Seng left. One of them said to me, "We want to acquire your Teng San Brickworks. We want you to make bricks for us and we will pay you."

There was no debate about it. They just put up a signboard, saying "Controlled by the Airforce" outside the brickworks. And that was that.

The Japanese kept a close watch on the factory. The soldiers would arrive early in the morning and sit in the office until the work was finished. They kept a record of how many bricks were produced and at the end of the month, we went by their figure. If they said they'd taken away half-a-million bricks, we calculated how much for each brick, charging them whatever we liked in a bill we submitted to the Japanese Air Force. They paid me without bargaining, because as far as they were concerned they were getting the bricks for free. You see, they issued military scrip that they printed at their whim and fancy. By the end of the war the currency had no value. It was nothing more than wastepaper.

My family's only source of income during the Occupation was that factory. They had already requisitioned our other brickworks at Alexandria, for which they did not pay us a cent. They made use of the Alexandria factory until the whole thing collapsed.

But the biggest blow was what they did to our brand new biscuit factory. We had invested more than $300,000 to acquire the latest machinery from England for a biscuit factory, the latest on the island. That was a fortune in those days and the same capital would cost millions today.

The Japanese put up a sign saying, "Controlled", outside the factory. They locked the place, stationed armed guards outside and stripped the whole factory down to the last nut and bolt so they could reassemble it in Thailand to supply biscuits to their army in Burma. Just like that.

Oh, they gave me some Japanese scrip for it, but it was quite useless. It was no compensation for the capital we had invested. Even after the war, I should have made a claim for compensation but I wasn't aware that there was such compensation available. Now I look at all those tycoons who had tiny little biscuit shops then and think of what I could have made with the equipment I had. If not for the Japanese.

But one has to count one's blessings. At least we had the Teng San Brickworks. If not for that, we would have been dead. We'd have had to resort to black-marketing and all the dangers associated with it.

Also, because the Japanese depended on our brickworks, they agreed to my request for rations for the workers. I insisted that my labourers could not work if their stomachs were empty. They saw the rationale to that. That was really lucky. Or else how could I have recruited workers? The Japanese supplied rations of rice, cooking oil, salt and sugar for the labourers and my family. I think, all in, the rations supported at least 300 people.

They also allowed me to have a car. I had a Fiat before the Occupation, but during the chaos of war, the British refused to let us drive across a certain line and I was forced to abandon it. I never saw it again. I was left with an old Morris. It was an antique even then. The Japanese gave me a permit, which I had to display on the windscreen. It was black in colour. The black permit was an ultimate luxury because it meant you could drive just about anywhere and consume any amount of petrol. Only those who the Japanese considered were contributing essential services got a black permit. If you had a red permit, you received a petrol ration.

Soon after the Japanese took over, a Taiwanese by the name of Wee Twee Kim approached the Chinese leaders and asked them, "What are you going to offer the Japanese?"

To save their necks, the businessmen made an offer of $50 million to the Japanese. A big sum, that was. But if they had offered a smaller sum, the Japanese may have felt offended and cut their heads off. So it was decided that $50 million was an acceptable sum.

The Chinese who promised the Japanese the money were smart. They knew that the local businessmen would not cough up a contribution willingly. What they did was they went to the Registrar of Companies and got hold of the list of all private limited companies and their stated paid-up capital. Then they declared that we had to contribute 5 per cent of our paid-up capital. In my family's case, our paid-up capital was $1 million. So we had to cough up $50,000. They sent us a bill saying so.

I was in two minds about paying up. Some friends kept telling me, "Don't pay-*lah*. They won't kill you."

But on the other hand, there were also rumours circulating that if you didn't comply, they would behead you. So in the end I thought, why risk my neck? Since I was in a position to pay, I might as well. And so I paid up. It took me a few months, with payments made in instalments.

Our family had to sell stocks of sugar and flour that we had stored up for the biscuit factory on the black market to raise the $50,000.

There were wealthy merchants who could afford to pay us for these goods and hoard them until the price went through the roof. Then, when they found that they could make, say, a 200 per cent profit, they sold some of the goods and kept the remainder, waiting for inflation to push prices even higher. They kept themselves going that way. I suppose they had families to support too.

By the time we raised the $50,000, we had nothing left. We were at the mercy of the Japanese rations. On reflection, I should have just refused to pay up. What could they have done? If you can't pay, you can't pay.

At the beginning, the soldiers who came to the factory were a very fierce lot. They shouted at us because we didn't understand them. Later, we got used to each other and they became friendlier. I even managed to pick up some Japanese from them.

After a time, I was approached by a Japanese civilian, Fukuda, who said, "When you deal with the Japanese, you'd better let me take charge. Come, let me help you, and you give me some money every month."

I thought it was better to have a Japanese to liaise with the military. So I said, "Okay, you take charge."

I paid him a fee every month. He came only occasionally, because he was in charge not only of my factory, but some sawmills elsewhere. Apart from Fukuda and the soldiers at my factory, I did not mix with the Japanese.

There was no opportunity for social mixing anyway. But even with our limited contact, we could tell that their attitude changed when they started losing the war. They were more civil, they didn't slap you about.

As the Occupation years dragged on, things began settling down to a familiar routine. It was then that I received news of my brother's whereabouts. He was in Perak when I got word that he was going to return. I was told not to tell the family, so I did not even tell his wife. My brother arrived with four others by submarine and travelled about on the island, with the Japanese completely unaware of their presence.

We were starved for news about the war, though. We had a little radio that we tuned in to secretly, late at night. It gave us news from India. We also got the *Syonan News*, which was basically a propaganda broadcast by the Japanese. But we could read between the lines and draw our own conclusions. If they said the Japs had a victory in the southeast islands, then we knew it meant the fighting was coming closer.

My brother died in 1944. Eventually, everybody working with him against the Japs was arrested. But I did not tell his wife. I was told not to inform anybody at all.

The Japanese Occupation split up my family. We were a very close-knit family, but when two-thirds of the family's business was out of operation, we had no choice but to split up. Everybody had to go their own way and make their own living. And in terms of business, of course, the Japanese wiped out a major portion of our capital.

Beheading became such a common occurrence that I became immune to the barbarism of the whole thing.

— Honorary President of the Malay Chamber of Commerce, Mohammad Ghazali Caffoor.

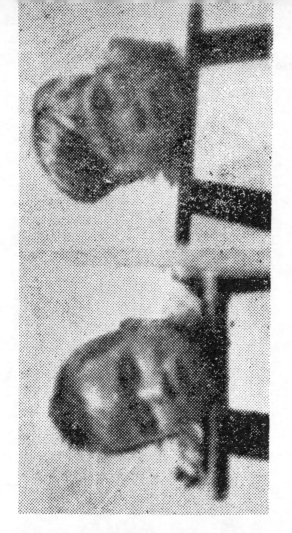

· 祭頭人之街哇小坡隆吉 ·

Heads of looters displayed at a road junction

Meeting Mohammad Ghazali Caffoor

Even though his father had a licence from the Japanese to run a restaurant at Stamford Road and the family had ample rations as a result, Mr Mohammad Ghazali Caffoor's story of how his father had a narrow escape at the hands of a drunken Japanese customer is a chilling reminder of how quickly one's luck could turn during the Occupation.

Mr Caffoor's description of drunken, carousing Japanese soldiers also belies the image of the humourless paragons of discipline that continue to dominate the popular myths. Conducting business with the Japanese soldiers could not have been an easy task for any trader, but catering to a rowdy crowd of carousing military men whose petulant will was the rule of law must surely have been a high-wire act without a net.

It was a fine line that Mr Caffoor, then only ten years old, helped his father walk, and soon found himself treading for different reasons. Apparently, the Japanese soldiers took a shine to him and wanted to adopt him as their mascot.

He lived to tell his story. Today, he is the Honorary President of the Malay Chamber of Commerce. Born in 1931, he has ten children, including a daughter who is married to a Japanese.

Facing the samurai sword

I was a boy of ten when Singapore jolted awake from the first Japanese air raid over the city.

My family lived in a brick bungalow along Changi Road then, but my father quickly evacuated the family to the safety of a kampung at Lorong Melayu. He felt we were safer there because it was more rural. In fact, a lot of people moved out of the city area to the undeveloped parts of Singapore during the invasion.

At Lorong Melayu we stayed with seven or eight other families in two houses that stood on a big plot of land. The families got together and built a bomb shelter of sorts. It was a rather crude shelter, just two holes in the ground with large planks pulled over them to protect us against stray shrapnel and the rain. If a bomb fell on us, we would have been wiped out.

Fortunately, we didn't get much action in our area during the invasion. But we did hear of bombs falling in Market Street and people shot dead with Sten guns around Kampung Batak.

I was not afraid of the Japanese when I met them for the first time because some of the people around me welcomed them. In the days before the Occupation, the Japanese sold very cheap products in Singapore, relative to British stores like Robinson's, so we were under the impression that if they took over, life would be easier. I could sense that some people welcomed the Japanese for that reason.

My father, who was about forty years old then, was very fluent in Japanese. He was a jeweller before the war and had travelled to Japan on business. Because of his fluency with the language and contacts with the Japanese, he was given a licence to run a Japanese restaurant at Stamford Road, near Capitol Cinema, during the Occupation. This gave us an opportunity to receive a steady supply of rice. We also distributed the rice among our relatives and friends.

I helped my father run his restaurant, which attracted hundreds of Japanese soldiers. When they were drunk, they behaved like animals. They fought and broke the furniture. The fights usually erupted over our ten or twelve waitresses, a mixed batch of Chinese, Eurasians and Indians.

In fact, my father almost lost his life trying to protect his staff. One episode occurred one night in 1943, at around 11 pm. A Japanese soldier, a fierce-looking officer, short and stout, with a long sword, had been drinking. He was unhappy with my father who asked him to stop harassing a waitress. The soldier asked my father to step out from the kitchen, telling him, "I want to talk to you."

My father said, "Wait, wait," and plied him with drinks. In the meantime, my father also tried to find another Japanese to challenge this fellow. He got hold of another Japanese soldier and said, "Please, you come, I want to talk to you."

Taking him to the kitchen, my father obliged him with lots of drinks and later, pointing out the other drunk officer, said, "You look, that man is trying to harm me."

When everybody else had left, my father persuaded the second officer in the kitchen to challenge the first drunkard. The two drunkards were soon spoiling for a fight. They started shoving each other. At this point, my father gently persuaded the second officer to take the fight outside.

So the two drunkards stumbled outside to a corner near Capitol Theatre. They drew out their swords and fought fiercely. Fortunately for my father, the second officer's reflexes were faster. In a moment of fury, he beheaded the other Japanese, whose head rolled into an uncovered drain. Frightened at what he had done, the surviving officer took off.

The next morning, the *Kempeitai* came to our restaurant to investigate.

First, they questioned the manager. My father had already told him to say he didn't know anything except that the two soldiers did indeed have a few drinks and leave.

Next, the *Kempeitai* hauled up my father for interrogation. He gave them same story. A Ceylonese chap called Dol, who spoke Japanese very fluently and worked with the *Kempeitai*, knew my father and took it onto himself to explain away the episode. And that's how my father escaped.

If the *Kempeitai* had found that my father was in any way responsible for the fight, they would have hanged him.

Later, I went to Penang because my father thought it was not a good idea for me to stay in Singapore anymore. You see, as my Japanese language skills grew, I became very keen to show off. I mingled and joked with the soldiers who frequented our restaurant and the soldiers took a liking to me. They talked of taking me to Burma with them. They claimed it would be a good chance for me to see a new place.

Being a young boy, I was very adventurous and thought it would be fun to go to Burma. My father, on the other hand, was very concerned, especially as I was the only son in the family. So he packed me off to a relative's house in Kampung Gajah in Province Wellesley, near an army camp.

There, I was the top student in the Japanese language. I even acted in Japanese dramas and sang Japanese songs on radio. I still vividly remember those songs.

As my new home was close to an army camp, I naturally became involved with the Japanese. I bartered *gula melaka* that we made for their cigarettes, which were in great demand. Even as a child, I had a keen business sense and these opportunities allowed me to make quite a bit of money for a boy my age.

But I also recall the dark side of the Occupation. The Japanese soldiers were crude and they did not go by any specific rules and regulations. They did as they liked.

Everything was very arbitrary.

Once I actually saw the Japanese behead a looter.

It happened near the army camp. I heard a commotion and sneaked through the crowd to see what it was about. I found my uncle, the one I was staying with, pleading the case of a Chinese chap who had been caught looting. But the Japanese did not listen to him.

They tied the man's hands behind his back, put a bamboo pole under his chin and with one deft stroke of the sword, lopped his head off. The severed head bounced like a ping pong ball. The Japanese placed it at a road junction, with a board stating his crime.

They also beheaded a Malay man who was caught trying to steal something from their camp. It became such a common occurrence that I became immune to the barbarism of the whole thing.

Instead, we were caught up in the fight for survival, always looking for a good business opportunity to exploit. Most of the time, such opportunities centred around the Japanese. They were the ones with the money and the power. When they got used to me, the soldiers even allowed me to buy food for them. They trusted me to the extent that I was allowed to go in and out of their camp freely. There were nearly 2,000 soldiers stationed there.

Occasionally, I bribed the Japanese sentry at the camp with "*nankinami*", which was a delicacy made from groundnuts coated with sugar, so that I could sneak into the store and grab a few packet drinks, cooked eggs and rice and give them to the POWs who did manual labour there. It was a big risk I took. If the Japanese ever came to know of it, they would definitely have tortured me.

The POWs were very grateful. They would say, "Thank you, thank you very much." Even now when I visualise them, I still feel moved to tears by the pathetic appearance of those starving, grateful POWs. You just cannot take it as a human being to see others suffer so much misery. (At this point Mr Caffoor began to cry and had to stop the interview to wipe his tears with a handkerchief.)

I had a close call one day when the camp could not account for ten missing bags of rice. An officer came to my uncle's house at night and interrogated me. He tried to intimidate me into confessing to the crime. It was a frightful experience for a boy my age. I shook and wept, but stuck to my guns. Eventually, a senior officer who was very fond of me came to know of this and he put an abrupt stop to it.

When the Japanese surrendered, they left me a bunch of keys to their store and told me to take whatever I wanted before the British moved in and confiscated everything. I took things like light bulbs, which I later sold. Six months later I moved back to Singapore. Things had changed. People moved around freely, looking for jobs and trying to piece their lives back together.

The climate of fear had evaporated.

I started my life anew.

I was only seventeen at the time and thought the war was exciting.

— Former Social Affairs Minister Othman Wok on the air raids.

An air-raid shelter during a Japanese attack

The overseas experience

For various reasons, some Singaporeans spent the unsettled years of the Japanese Occupation abroad. Some, like former Deputy Prime Minister Dr Toh Chin Chye were lucky enough to be repatriated by the Japanese to their hometowns in the Malayan Peninsula.

Others escaped to safe havens further away, like Mr Ameer Jumabhoy, who recounts how he had to sleep with a knife under his pillow en route to India and the close shave his ship had with a Japanese submarine.

Yet others were sent away, like Dr Lee Siew Choh, who is no stranger to Singaporeans. The charismatic veteran opposition politician survived the notorious Death Railway.

The Japanese recruited civilians from Singapore from 1943 for the Burma-Thailand Railway they were building. The first lot of about 200 labourers were said to have gone voluntarily in May 1943, lured by the promise of high wages. Those that followed in the next few months were also said to be volunteers.

Dr Lee, however, paints a different story.

A total of 600 civilians from Singapore are believed to have gone to the Death Railway, so called because many people, especially POWs died of disease and exhaustion building it.

Another group of people who left Singapore went

at the instigation of the Japanese to set up self-sufficient agricultural communities in Malaya so that they could relieve the population pressure in Singapore, which had become critical by August 1943, leading to food shortages and rising discontent.

One group was made up of Chinese who raised $1 million to build a settlement at Endau in Johor. By September 1944, there were 12,000 settlers in what was described as a "Chinese Utopia". Food production was good, as was general health, and the settlement did well despite some guerilla attacks. After the war, though, the settlement was abandoned as city-loving Singaporeans decided it was safe to come back.

Not so lucky were the Roman Catholics from Singapore who set up two communities at Bahau under the leadership of Bishop Devals. Particularly depressed were the Eurasian Catholics. They had a poorer site than the Chinese Catholics who set up in the valley.

Mr George Bogaars, the former head of the Singapore Civil Service, describes life at Bahau for the Eurasians. His keen mind and sharp memory provide a good idea of life for the estimated one-fifth of the Eurasian community of Singapore, who settled there.

Meeting Dr Toh Chin Chye

Dr Toh Chin Chye really needs no introduction as he is a household name. His political career as a founder-member of the ruling People's Action Party and Deputy Prime Minister to outspoken backbencher critic has been well-documented and without a doubt, closely followed by Singaporeans. Suffice it then to say that after his retirement from politics Dr Toh still keeps extremely busy as an advisor to a major local corporation.

Described as a humble, honest and friendly man by his colleagues — when I met him at his office, he fit the description perfectly. He is still very much a people's man, concerned that the younger generation of Singaporeans have forgotten the history of their country, particularly the experiences and developments of World War Two.

Here, he shares his experience during that period when he was, in the words of a colleague, "A young, science student in Raffles College in white overalls — studious, serious-minded."

The outbreak and aftermath of the war changed all that and propelled him into the political arena. As Dr Toh says, it "ignited political consciousness in all of us".

College student caught in the crossfire

I grew up in a multi-racial environment, studying in a school run by Catholic missionaries in Taiping and later in a Methodist school in Ipoh.

As schools grew, the demand for English language teachers rose. In 1939 I applied for and was awarded a Federal Government scholarship to study in Raffles College in Singapore. The students from Malaya lived together in the hostel. The Singapore students were non-hostelites having little interaction with us.

When World War Two broke out in Europe, we read about it in the press. But we were oblivious of the political impact it would have on Malaya and Singapore where we were part of the British Empire on which the sun never set. Then one day we read of the need for air-raid shelters to be built in Singapore and to organise Air-Raid Prevention (ARP) Corps. As hostelites, we were mobilised and went through drills on rescue operations.

We knew of the Japanese Occupation of China but had no inkling that the threat to Malaya and Singapore would come from the East. The European war in any case was so distant. There were, however, reports of trade tensions between Japan and the West and the "toing and froing" of Japanese envoys to Washington. This turned out to be the prelude to Japanese entry into World War

Two.

It was two days before my twentieth birthday when the first bombs fell on Singapore in the middle of the night. The Japanese also made the Singapore Naval Base ineffective by sinking the main naval warships that were supposed to protect Singapore. Soon, Japanese troops were landing on the beaches of Kuantan. Their advance was swift as their airforce held supremacy in the skies.

As casualties mounted, we were switched from the ARP to the Medical Auxiliary Service (MAS) to attend to the wounded. One month later, the Japanese crossed the Johor Straits and the battlefront was pushed towards the city. Medical supplies started to run out. I remember two hefty persons were asked to hold a wounded man down while the doctor removed a piece of shrapnel from his leg without anaesthesia. I heard the screams coming from the makeshift operating theatre.

Troops could be seen around the Botanic Gardens and one evening, my unit was ordered to leave our base at Raffles College for the Singapore General Hospital (SGH). We were posted to the Chemistry Department within the grounds of the SGH, overlooking Outram Road. Further down at the opposite end of the road was a landmark, Outram Road Prison, which no longer exists.

The situation at the SGH was chaotic as the casualties mounted and spilled over into the Medical College building. Some of them were shell shocked. They convulsed or screamed whenever a shell whistled overhead, as the area came under mortar fire. The whistling of approaching shells was scary. We were sitting ducks crouching behind a barricade of sandbags, waiting and guessing where the shells would land.

One of the shells exploded just outside our quarters but fortunately nobody was injured. Others were not that lucky. A group of medical students working in the SGH were killed by mortar fire and they were buried in a mass grave with other civilian casualties. The grave is still there next to the car park in the SGH.

By this time, the water supply had been cut off and when our British officers vanished, we knew that the war had been lost. We were left to fend for ourselves.

The next morning, from our vantage viewpoint we saw streams of civilians walking along Outram Road towards the town. I learnt later that it was a mass round-up for screening.

Being in the MAS probably saved me and my companions as the Japanese hustled us to another hospital in Lim Chu Kang to attend to wounded British prisoners of war. There, we were given rations that were inadequate or inedible and we were forced to swap our remaining dollars for food from the villagers across the barbed wire. Discipline was tight and we were not allowed to wander around the hospital.

After the battle for Singapore was over, we still felt the aftereffects. When it rained, it rained soot coming from the fuel tanks that continued to burn from the earlier bombing and shelling. When water was partially restored, we took turns to wash ourselves at a roadside standpipe.

This was a luxury we were allowed only once a week.

About two months later, everybody in the hospital who came from Malaya was packed like sardines into a goods train on a slow, hot journey home. My family had heard about the battle for Singapore and did not expect me to return.

After the initial rejoicing at being reunited, we settled down to eke out a living under the Japanese Occupation. Pre-war currency was withdrawn and replaced by Japanese issue of "banana notes". As imports came to a standstill, food and goods became scarce and prices climbed. I became an assistant to a vegetable hawker in a wet market but his capital dwindled with inflation and the business closed. What I had studied had no application. It would have been better if I had taken a course in how to be streetwise.

I subsequently studied Japanese and taught it in a school. In return, I was paid in cash, rice and cigarettes. The cigarettes, though locally made, were a luxury item which I sold on the black market.

Malaria and malnutrition were rife then. We used tapioca to supplement our rice ration. It was really an art cooking tapioca with rice. The tapioca was first grated, and then washed to remove traces of vegetable cyanide. Everybody planted tapioca on any open piece of land. In fact, the Japanese organised teachers and civil servants to plant tapioca on public land.

Smoking opium was permitted and the Japanese encouraged gambling. When squabbles broke out in the gambling parks, a squad from the Japanese garrison descended on it to restore order. They also used it as an opportunity to detain anti-Japanese elements.

The Chinese took the brunt of punishment from the Japanese military. This was because we were regarded as sympathisers of Chiang Kai Shek or of the Malayan People's Anti-Japanese Alliance (MPAJA), which had initiated a jungle guerilla warfare against the Occupation.

We, the population, were caught in the crossfire between the Japanese military and the MPAJA. There were informers for the *Kempeitai* and underground workers for the MPAJA. Stories on how the *Kempeitai* tortured their prisoners leaked out and created an air of oppression. Conversation with strangers became cautious.

The days dragged, with the value of paper money falling everyday. Then, one afternoon, an aeroplane flew low over the town. It was the British. They dropped leaflets which we rushed to collect as if dollars were raining from the sky. The leaflets promised that liberation would not be far away.

But it was many months before liberation finally came. The first official indication I got that the Japanese Occupation was coming to an end was when the principal gathered all the teachers and informed us that the school was to be closed.

As the Japanese garrison withdrew, a platoon of the MPAJA paraded through the town. It was a motley crowd of people, some armed and in uniform, while others were not. They took control of the town as the British had not yet arrived. It was a period of lawlessness and revenge was taken on those suspected to have worked as informers for the *Kempeitai*.

The MPAJA was really headed by the Malayan Communist Party (MCP). The end of the war brought the MCP into prominence as it tried to wrest political power. But its Marxist-Leninist doctrine was foreign to the population at large. Even worse, its dominant Chinese character antogonised the Malays, who formed the majority of the population.

Having failed to gain political legitimacy, the MCP did what it knew best. It returned to guerilla warfare, this time against the British. This was how the Emergency began, with the first shots fired at British planters in Sungei Siput in Perak. The MCP found itself fighting against an elected Malayan government and the futile armed struggle formally ended only forty-one years later in 1989.

For all of us, the war and its aftermath ignited political consciousness, as we followed the divesting of the British Empire.

There was a
climate of
oppression.
Like the
Japanese
sentry... you
had to get
past him
everyday.

— Former head of
the civil service,
George Bogaars.

Japanese sentry checking a young man's pass

Meeting George Bogaars

"I'm no Churchill," was Mr George Bogaars' first response when I telephoned him, seeking an interview.

But his story must be told. He has led a long and illustrious life as a senior civil servant who was deeply involved in the shaping of post-war Singapore. Eventually he became the head of the Civil Service.

His father, G. E. Bogaars Senior, served as a confidential secretary to four British Governors, including Sir Shenton Thomas.

The younger Bogaars received his early education at St Patrick's School and St Joseph's Institution. Then came the war, when Mr Bogaars relocated with his family and a substantial portion of the Eurasian community to the Bahau Settlement in Negri Sembilan.

"As for the impact of the war on me personally, it can be summed up in one sentence: When the Japanese came to Singapore, I was a boy; when they left, I was a young man," says Mr Bogaars.

His recollection of life in Bahau is unusually detailed, considering that the experience occurred about fifty years ago. Mr Bogaars had one of the keenest memories among all the interviewees, recalling such details as the size of the communal hut that he lived in.

After the war, he went on to read History at the

University of Malaya in Singapore, graduating with a Master's degree in 1952. He wanted to teach, but his father insisted that he join the administrative service.

"My father, a colonial civil servant all his life, had a very British outlook. Anyway, I was getting on in years so everything was conspiring to get me to join," said Mr Bogaars.

He joined the civil service immediately after graduating at the age of twenty-six and proved a high-flyer. Within three years, he rose to the position of acting deputy secretary in the Treasury.

The Malayanisation of the civil service was going on apace at the time and it was a period he looked back on with relish. "I believe you had to have that feeling that there was a national task to do, to take over the administration of the country from the expatriates, as it were. Young men had that feeling. This was quite a strong motivating factor. We felt there was a job to be done."

He became the first Singaporean to head the Special Branch, the forerunner of the present Internal Security Department. He led Operation Coldstore on February 2, 1963, which involved the round-up of 114 left-wingers. When Singapore became independent in 1965, he became the permanent secretary to the Ministry of Interior and Defence and played a major role in the build-up of Singapore's young armed forces. He also helped set up the Singapore Armed Forces Training Institute, known as Safti.

"It's something I feel quite happy about. We created something that had not existed before and made it into an institution that produces good officers," he says.

Mr Bogaars became the head of the Civil Service in 1968, and stepped down only in 1975 when he went back to the Finance Ministry as a permanent secretary. He left the civil service in 1981 at the age of fifty, but continued an active working life, taking over the helm of Keppel Shipyard and National Iron and Steel Mills as their chairman.

Mr Bogaar's stint at Keppel Shipyard was a controversial one, marred partly by the Sentosa cable car disaster of January, 1983. In March 1985, he suffered a mild heart attack and had a stroke that left him numb on the left side of his face and affected his vision. He lost 25 kg in a few months. Mr Bogaars started easing out of his senior positions that year.

Today he lives alone, with a maid to take care of him. He is surrounded in his private apartment by clocks and timepieces of several shapes and sizes, reflecting a fascination he has carried with him since childhood. He is not well physically, but his mind is still sharp as a razor. He spends most of his time in physiotherapy, but his strength and determination are self-evident. To listen to him talk in his understated manner, it slowly dawns on you how he could have survived such a devastating experience in Bahau. And how he carries on today...

Mr Bogaars is divorced from his wife. He has two daughters and one son.

It rained soot from the fuel tanks that burned from the bombing and shelling.

— Former Deputy Prime Minister Dr Toh Chin Chye on the aftereffects of the battle for Singapore.

Fire fighters struggling to cope after a Japanese air raid

Surviving Bahau

The night the Japanese first attacked Singapore, we were awakened by the rumble of aeroplanes and had no idea what was going on. There were rumours running through the whole neighbourhood that night, but no one ever suspected that the Japanese had bombed us until the next morning when we read about it in the newspapers. My father continued to commute to work at Government House from our residence near St Patrick's School until it got too dangerous. Then the British moved us nearer to Government House, to quarters at Chancery Lane.

Staying there was dangerous too because the place was surrounded by important British installations that were Japanese targets. But we built an air-raid shelter for our safety. With the help of a gardener, we dug a trench in the side of the hill behind the house and covered it with steel and iron bars.

I struck on the idea of recording the frequency of the Japanese raids. You see, I had a passion for time the way most other kids were consumed by coins or stamps. And even then, I thought such a record could be useful someday for historical purposes. I managed to record the frequency of the raids until they became so intense and continuous that I just could not keep track.

Then we were pushed out of Chancery Lane by an

Australian artillery battery unit, which moved into our front garden without any ceremony or warning. The officer-in-charge told my parents it was advisable for us to flee because the Japanese were coming down Bukit Timah Road.

We became refugees. We took shelter at the Singapore General Hospital, which withstood many Japanese raids and was one of the most solid buildings around. They cleared out a few wards and all the refugee-types like us had to live there. The place was packed but we were fortunate to secure a space on the verandah of one of the wards.

There was bombing and shelling throughout the day. The hospital facilities were pathetically inadequate because the Japanese had got control of our water supply and the sheer over-crowding in the wards only compounded the problem. You couldn't bathe. Water was only for drinking, and even that was very limited. At one stage, there was just a trickle of water from the taps. We ate food from cans.

Fortunately for my family, my mother managed to get in touch with her brother-in-law, who was a doctor. We moved in with his family to the doctors' quarters at College Road.

On one occasion, a bomb fell just a few yards away from the quarters. We were lucky to survive the impact of the blast, but the quarters we had holed up in was wrecked.

So we moved again, this time to the Sin Chew Hospital in Victoria Street, where my mother's brother had a clinic. I think it is still standing today. That was where we were when the Japanese declared victory. It was not unexpected, as the rumour of surrender at Bukit Timah spread through the hospital a good few hours before the official announcement.

Japanese flags just sprung up from nowhere on people's doors. I presume there were commercially-minded chaps who exploited the situation.

Soon after the Japanese took over, they sealed off an area between Arab Street and North Bridge Road, near the hospital. From where we were staying, we could see hordes and hordes of Chinese being marched into the area. It appeared they were being screened, and in the evenings they used to take truckloads of Chinese out of the area. It must have dawned on many of these fellows what the screening was all about and some tried to escape. I saw two or three shot dead during the day by the Japanese sentries that patrolled the area.

It must have been much worse at night, presumably because most of them would have tried to escape under cover of darkness. I say this because we heard constant gunfire at night, but we did not dare investigate. We kept our windows bolted. The evidence was usually still there the next morning.

Soon after this episode, the Japanese turned their attention to the Eurasians. They issued a proclamation that all Eurasians had to assemble on the Padang in front of the Singapore Recreation Club for "registration". It sounded ambiguous and my parents were very apprehensive about their real motives, especially since we knew what they had done to the Chinese. And it was common knowledge that the Eurasians were very loyal to the British and so obviously suspect in their loyalty to the Japanese.

We really had no option but to go because there was such a lot of confusion after the surrender that we thought it was better to do as we were told. We went in the hope that the worst that would come about would be some form of internment.

In the event, most Eurasians were told to go home. My family too. Only those with European parentage were given a red star to wear.

A few weeks after the surrender, my family moved back to Chancery Lane. The place was a mess. It had been looted, there was a big carcass of rotting meat on the grounds, ammunition all over the place and even faeces.

Almost immediately after we moved in, we were visited by a stern, pint-sized Japanese officer in a big, military car. He asked my father to identify himself. And then they carted him off. I was a kid and didn't know what was going on, but my mother was very anxious.

In the evening, thankfully, my father returned. In reply to our questions, he told us how he was interrogated and told to write an essay about his life. But our ordeal was not over yet. My father had to report to the *Kempeitai* Headquarters at the old YMCA at Orchard Road for another four or five days, returning only in the evenings.

I think my father outwitted them. He gave them the impression that he was a low-level clerk in Government

House, who had no knowledge of anything of importance. In actual fact, he was well aware of all correspondence that was relayed between the Singapore Governor and London.

Ironically, while my father fought for his life with the Japanese, my brother and I developed an acquaintance with a Japanese lieutenant who was a tank commander stationed at the Anglo-Chinese School behind our house.

We stumbled across him when we heard him scrambling down the hill behind our house and went to see what the commotion was all about. Being a young chap, possibly in his early twenties, he was eager to make friends. He beckoned to us and when we went up to him, he held out a fistful of foreign coins, which he offered us. We became good friends. He was the first Japanese I had ever met.

But precisely because of his battalion stationed at the Anglo-Chinese School and the harassment and uncertainty my father faced with the *Kempeitai*, my parents decided it would be a good idea if we moved to my grandfather's house at St Francis Road. The area was safer because we would be unnoticed among a lot of local people. So we moved. But before we left, I got my Japanese friend to pen me his autograph. I kept it for a long time, but I don't know where it's gone now.

Life under the Japanese, as far as I can recollect, involved a great deal of dabbling in the black market. But of course, you needed to have money to get into the act. As far as my family was concerned, our main income was from goods we looted from other houses at Chancery Lane. There were a lot of abandoned houses in the premises with quite a few valuable things left behind like goods and cutlery. We, like the rest of Singapore, helped ourselves to these items. With these things, we bartered for other goods during the period we were at St Francis Road.

I remember there was a black marketeer who used to be friendly with us, a small-time Chinese businessman who lived at St Michael's Road. When he saw the goods, he quoted us a price for them. We made the transaction with him and I am sure he sold the things at a big profit. That was the way the market operated. My father also used to get a ration of cigarettes, which he didn't smoke fully; he used the surplus to trade on the black market for essentials like rice and sugar.

The official Japanese line was that black-marketing was taboo. But they themselves took part in it because it was the way of life then. There was a flourishing black market in Japanese cigarettes for one thing. Like most occupying armies, the Japanese had their own military goods and food which they flogged on the black market. The soldier got a small wage, but a big food ration. So he sold some of his ration on the black market. You can rest assured that there were people who contacted them and asked for things like canned pineapples or cigarettes. It was all a matter of contacts. Who you knew.

Apart from the shortage of food, there was also a climate of oppression. Like the Japanese sentry, for instance. You had to walk past him everyday once you stepped out of the house. If you were riding a bicycle, you had to dismount and bow to him. I was a witness to what happened to one poor fellow who didn't do it. He was tied to a lamppost and made to kneel there for the whole day. After that, they carted him away and God knows what happened to him. All for not bowing to the sentry.

My father was really anti-Japanese. He hated them. He refused to work for them and we were not even allowed to go to the Japanese schools or speak Japanese. He deliberately flaunted the laws they laid down. For instance, all radios were to be sealed and that meant we could listen only to the local broadcast that spouted Japanese propaganda.

My father broke the seal on our radio and tuned in to the BBC every night. He hid the radio in the laundry basket and ignored the threat of being beheaded by the Japanese if it was found. That is, until the *Kempeitai* raided our neighbour's house. The neighbours, also Eurasians, were very friendly with the Indian Nationalist Army, and the Japanese suspected them of some funny business. Fortunately they didn't come to our place. But my mother seized the opportunity to convince my father to bury the radio in the poultry barn. And that was the end of the BBC for us.

He also opposed simple things like sticking a Japanese flag out during the Emperor's birthday. Once again my mother had to fight hard before he reluctantly gave in.

When he heard about the Bahau project — a Catholic community settlement for Eurasians to live and farm in

Bahau, Negri Sembilan — he saw it as an opportunity to get away from Japanese rule. And, of course, he might have had a vision that it would be a good life. In fact, he became the secretary to Bishop Devals, who headed the whole project.

Generally, I recall a sort of holiday atmosphere among those who departed for Bahau with me and my brother in December 1943. By and large, the chaps were either leaving Singapore because they wanted to get away from the Japanese or because they thought it would be wonderful in Bahau. There was a mood of festivity on the train that took us to Bahau town.

However, the merrymaking came to an abrupt halt when we reached the settlement. My first impression of Bahau was one of horror. First and foremost, we had to trudge with all our belongings for a quarter of a mile to the settlement as the truck that ferried us there was unable to progress any further because there was no proper road leading to the settlement. Even walking was not easy as the path was muddy and slippery because it had rained for sometime before our arrival.

At the settlement itself, things were just as stark. There was no privacy. No luxuries.

We were housed in a long hut, the community hut. The centre of the hut was a platform about ten feet wide, and four feet off the ground. That was where we lived. We were each given a space of about six by four feet to store all our belongings. We slept head to head on a platform of planks that substituted for beds and pillows.

Everything was done communally. Cooking, eating, bathing. Everything.

Every morning, at about seven or seven-thirty, there was a roll call. Then we started with the community work. It consisted of hard labour, including building a proper road to the settlement. There was also the cooking and the digging of toilets for the community. It was hard for us. My brother and I were not used to this kind of life.

The land was completely undeveloped. They had simply felled the jungle and sent the young men of the Eurasian community in. There were logs all over the place that had to be cleared or burnt. It was not a place for the women or the elderly.

To compensate, the Japanese gave the settlers six months supply of subsistence rations. Within the six months, one had to build one's house and grow enough food to survive because after that period you received no ration and how you survived was your business.

To make it worse, the land allotted to the Eurasians was not suitable for cultivation. The Japanese had built two such settlements, one for the Chinese Catholics and the other for the Eurasian Catholics. The Chinese were at the third mile, the Eurasians at the fifth. The Chinese, either through luck or skill, got the better land. It was in the valley, where it rained frequently and was therefore well-watered. The Eurasians got the hilly area. More importantly, water was difficult to obtain. It must have appealed to the Japanese sense of humour because they called our settlement, Fuji-go, saying it resembled the famous mountain.

The Chinese grew rice, whereas even the most successful of farms in Bahau simply couldn't grow this essential staple food. If we were lucky, we managed to grow Indian corn, tapioca, sugar cane; they did not need too much water. At one point the Japanese even encouraged us to plant cotton for the seed oil, either for lubrication or something to do with the war effort. We were issued a whole lot of cotton seeds and asked to plant them, but that was not a very successful attempt.

With no experience in construction, my brother and I could not build a hut for our family. So when the rest of the family came to Bahau in the middle of 1944, my father had to pay a contractor $300 to construct a crude hut with three partitions for our family of five; inclusive of my sister and mother. It took the contractor four months to construct it and the family had to rough it out in the community hut till then.

Even after moving into our own hut, life was difficult. We had to sink two wells, one of which was perpetually dry. The other well was not too bad, but it meant carrying the water 100 yards to the house every day. Food was insufficient and we had to barter a lot of our belongings like bedsheets and clothes with the villagers around Bahau in return for simple necessities like sugar and rice. We even resorted to laying traps in the jungle to catch animals like wild fowl, mouse deer and wood pigeons. And even then, we had to contend with a hungry settler who stole our game.

Looking back I would say that it would have been impossible for the city folk of Singapore to survive the rigours of Bahau if not for their sheer determination and spirit.

Out of the 3,000 people that went to Bahau, thirty per cent of them perished, many from malaria that plagued us throughout our stay. Even the most able-bodied fell prey to the disease and if you could fight it off once, there was no guarantee that it would not recur. In fact, repeated attacks of malaria were the order of the day there. It was called black-water fever and it crippled the brain. One had to take large doses of quinine religiously as a prophylactic in order to ward off the menace. As hungry as we were, quinine tasted horridly bitter. Even in its normal form it was a task to swallow. It was doubly worse in liquid form, which was how it was supplied.

Partly because of malaria, the Japanese left us much to ourselves. They were also afraid of the anti-Japanese guerillas who were operating in the area. The only time I remember them showing up was to round up the able-bodied chaps to work at clearing a jungle area called Ladang Geddes on which they planned to build an air strip. Fortunately that went on only for some six months or so.

It was impossible to escape from Bahau. The first obstacle was the sheer isolation of the camp. In those days it was not easy to move around. One needed special authorisation. I doubt we would have got the authorisation to return to Singapore because then we would have been able to spread the real truth of the horror of Bahau. The settlers, who continued arriving right up to the end, would have been put off. That was why the Allies considered us prisoners of war when they moved in.

Up there, we were entirely cut off from the outside world. I didn't know of anyone with a radio. Towards the end of the war, though, we saw Allied bombers flying over us, presumably to bomb Singapore. I recall them dropping some leaflets in Bahau. I think it was one of those "Keep your spirits up" kind of leaflets that briefly mentioned the progress of war on the Burma front.

Our first confirmation of Allied victory was when the guerillas came out of the jungle and set up their headquarters in the settlement. They requisitioned our only truck and brought food from Kuala Pilah, keeping in touch with the Allies by radio.

One day, the settlers were told that on a certain day of the week in the evening, between about five and six o'clock, we were to light a few bonfires because the Americans were going to drop food supplies. We did as we were told and were rewarded with six huge canisters, six or eight feet long, with plenty of provisions. They included things like fresh bread and milk powder — luxuries most of us had not tasted for three-and-a-half years.

After four such drops, parachuters landed. A major and three other soldiers. They took complete control of the settlement, established wireless contact with Singapore and kept us informed about general matters. They told us the Japanese were leaving Malaya and we could soon return to Singapore.

That was the one time the Bahau settlement rang with festivities — the way we had imagined it would when we first came. The surviving settlers organised dances. We celebrated the end of the nightmare.

It was a real surprise the way the Japanese surrendered quietly and peacefully. We had thought they would fight to the end and take the whole population with them.

The major preoccupation for me during the Japanese Occupation was food. We were all the time hungry, constantly thinking of food. As for the impact of the war on me personally, it can be summed up in one sentence: when the Japanese came to Singapore, I was a boy; when they left I was a young man.

When you depend on your parents, you have childish ideas. You think life is one big holiday. By the time the Japanese left, I jolly well knew that life was more than a holiday. I could stand on my own two feet and I was confident in the knowledge that in any situation I would be okay.

When the British returned, there wasn't the same climate of fear as under the Japanese.

— Veteran politician Dr Lee Siew Choh on the return of the Allied troops.

Welcoming back the Allied troops

Meeting Dr Lee Siew Choh

Not many people know that veteran politician Dr Lee Siew Choh was a survivor of the notorious Death Railway.

Born in 1917 in Kuala Lumpur, he arrived in Singapore in 1936 to study medicine. He was a young, unmarried, graduate doctor working at Kandang Kerbau Hospital, living in the doctors' quarters with his mother and sister when the Japanese took over.

About a year into the Occupation, Dr Lee was unceremoniously picked to test his fate on the infamous Death Railway. The idea of building a railway from Thailand to Burma had occurred to the British long before the Second World War. However, as calculations revealed that the cost in terms of human lives would be staggering in that malaria-ridden jungle belt, they abandoned the plan.

During the Occupation, however, when the Japanese were being pulverised around the Indian Ocean and the Malacca Straits, they decided to supply their forces in Burma by land, by building a railway from Thailand to Rangoon.

Apart from the prisoners of war, thousands of Indians, Malays and Chinese from Malaya and thousands more Javanese were sent daily to this harbour of disease as labourers to do their part for the noble Co-Prosperity Sphere. An estimated 130,000 people perished on the lines, giving the Death Railway its deserved name.

Most accounts were given by former prisoners of war and Dr Lee's is one of the few available from a local perspective. Fortunately for him, he was not sent to the front line where the worst casualties occurred.

After the war, Dr Lee became quite active in politics and his career is well chronicled. Suffice to say that today Dr Lee, who has four children, runs a modest medical practice, often answering his own phone calls. He is very approachable and immediately gives you the impression of one who has been through much in life, but will not easily let the fire in his belly die.

"At one point, the building next to my hospital quarters was bombed," says Dr Lee. Yes, he has seen the face of death and walked away. But that was not his only escape. He was to cheat the Grim Reaper two more times during the Occupation, but let him tell his own story...

The Death Railway Experience

When the war broke out in 1941, I had just graduated as a doctor and was stationed at the Kandang Kerbau Hospital. At that time it was called the General Hospital and I was staying in the compound where they had the doctors' quarters, together with my mother and sister.

It was a frightful time for us. There were many air raids. It became so continuous that you could not differentiate one air raid from another. Hospitals were a main target of the Japanese. The quarters next to mine was bombed and there were plenty of casualties. As a doctor, I was in the thick of things, treating casualties of the war as the General Hospital was for civilians.

Nobody knew what was going to happen then. There was general confusion and panic. When we read in the papers that the Prince of Wales and the Repulse had been sunk, we were shocked that such huge ships could go down so easily. The British were saying otherwise but we could see that the Japanese were strong and the British could not measure up to them.

We were very angry with the British then. The way they treated us and threw their weight around, they obviously didn't care much for the civilians. One particular incident stands out for me. We were all huddled up in our quarters during an air raid when one of these British captains came in and started shouting at us and threatening us if we did not listen to orders. It was totally unnecessary. He was armed and showing off and it was clearly an abuse of power. And at such a time too. It was unforgiveable. Instead of wanting to help him, we just felt resentment.

When the Japanese took over and the *sook ching* began, I escaped because I remained in the hospital. I didn't follow the orders to go to a certain area for screening. I sensed that something was going to happen there. The Japanese expected everyone to obey once the order was given because people were so fearful of them, who would dare disobey? But if I had gone out, I may not be here today, I don't know. Some of my friends went and I never heard from them again. One doctor went. Never came back. My wife's brother went; never came back.

I continued to stay at the hospital quarters at Kandang Kerbau, although by then the Japanese had taken over the place. There were Japanese sentries at the entrance of the hospital. They were quite friendly chaps actually. I guess it was because the war was over and they were not front line soldiers. I recall how we had to study Japanese at Kandang Kerbau. We were given books and had teachers. And then we practised whatever we had learnt on the guards. I was quite good at it at one time.

After about a year or so, the Japanese gave orders that about a dozen doctors from Kandang Kerbau were to go to the Death Railway in Thailand. They gave their orders through the then medical superintendant of the hospital, Doctor Benjamin Sheares, who later became President of Singapore. I suppose he had no choice but to comply and unfortunately I was one of those picked to go. We really had no alternative. We had to do as we were told. It was an order.

One day, together with about twelve other doctors, I was herded onto a cattle truck. Luckily the truck was covered so we at least had some shelter. It took us a good few days to get up there and on the very first day of our arrival at our destination, we were nearly blasted to smithereens by the Allies.

There were a number of stations along that railway. I was posted to the main station of Kanchinaburi. Other doctors were sent further up north. Our duty was to look after the non-European, non-Japanese workers. There were lots of labourers from Java as well as Malays, some Chinese and many Indians from Singapore. The Japanese, of course, had their own Japanese doctor to look after them.

We were not treated too badly. We had some form of communication with the doctor and the commander of the camp. But there was always the fear of what they might or might not do. Sometimes, the guards would suddenly walk into our quarters, look around, check how things were. But we didn't have a clandestine radio or anything like that, so we were all right. The guards treated us comparatively well. They never hit us or anything like that, but the fear was always there because they were very free with their hands and slaps with the others, see? That's how it was.

The Japanese provided meals for us. Twice a day. But, of course, it was not good food. The best meal we ever had was fish. Once a week, though, we were allowed to go into the village, which was a little distance away. We could get a good Thai meal there.

We were given a small monthly salary in Thai currency and we used it to buy things on the thriving Thai black market. We had to look out for ourselves and make sure we had enough to survive. It was a natural instinct. We were very sparing with the rations that we were given in camp and we exchanged the surplus for things like rice on the black market. Rice was, of course, the hottest item on the market. It was difficult communicating with the Thai villagers but eventually we picked up a few key Thai words like "where to", "how much money" and things like that to get by.

(Ed: Dr Lee had not read Russell Braddon's book, The Naked Island, but I put to him Braddon's position that the Westerners were much more self-reliant and more optimistic about their situation in Kanchinaburi than the Asians, who Braddon said "were not blessed with the moral fibre to stand up against difficulties".)

I don't think it was a case of lacking a fighting spirit. We just did our job and hoped for the best. That's all. We never thought about how it was going to end. It was a question of concentrating on surviving each day.

The labourers were just, you know, pushed around, and they hoped for the best under the circumstances. I spoke to many of them. They didn't dare talk about the war or how they expected it to end or things like that because if they were caught saying anything against the Japanese, they would have got it.

I had been there about nine months when talk of the Japanese surrender was whispered about. It was in the air. You could just sense it. We were stunned at how quickly it all ended. When we heard about the atom bomb, we thought it was a wonderful thing. But later, of course, when the news became clearer we realised that wasn't true.

With the surrender, we were allowed to go back to Singapore. Together with all the survivors, I rushed back to my family. The journey home was one of a kind. At some points, we actually had to get out of the train with all our belongings strapped to us and push the train because the tracks were not firm enough.

I brought back some Thai savings with me. At that time, I think the exchange rate was one to seven or one to eight. I was hoping it would go up so I held on to it. But it became useless. In the end, I threw it away.

When the British returned, there wasn't the same climate of fear anymore as under the Japanese. But they continued to treat us like second and third class citizens, whereas we already had it in our minds that the British were not too much better than the Japanese. They thought they were still masters and we their subjects but things eventually had to be reassessed.

All the nice cabins were taken by the wives of Britishers. We natives slept on deck.

— Businessman
A. Jumabhoy who
escaped from
Singapore by ship.

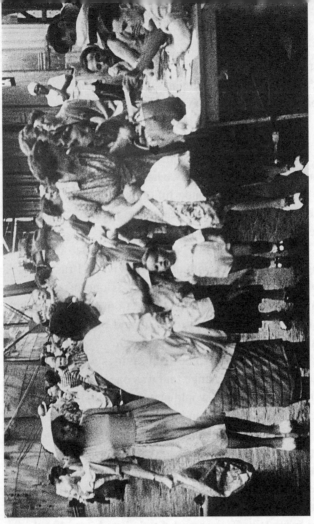

Europeans evacuate Singapore by ship

Meeting Ameer Jumabhoy

Fifty years ago, a teenager named Ameer slept with a dagger under his pillow, just in case he needed to protect his mother and younger brothers from drunken soldiers loitering outside the family home. Today, as chairman of the multimillion-dollar Scotts Group of Companies, Mr Ameerali Rajabali Jumabhoy employs an army of security guards just to protect his family business.

But Mr Jumabhoy, a very forceful personality, does not like his story to sound too sensational as he and his father — the latter having written a book about his life and experiences during the war — have had bad experiences with filmmakers and such, distorting the facts to fit their agenda.

Suffice then to note that Mr Jumabhoy's account of his escape from Singapore before the fall of the Fortress includes an eyewitness account of British soldiers presumably deserting their posts to escape with their wives on board the ships meant for Indian refugees.

Mr Jumabhoy's own escape was made possible by his father's strong connections to the British elite. Shortly before the war, his father, R. Jumabhoy, already a successful businessman, was the Municipal Commissioner of Singapore. During the war, he was a member of the British Military Advisory Council.

The younger Jumabhoy returned to Singapore after the war and joined his father's business in 1949, when he was seventeen. He married in 1950 and has four children.

Today he is chairman of the Scotts Group, which is greatly diversified and has interests in the leisure and lifestyle industry, retail stores, food and beverage, fast food, hospitality and shipping industries.

Fleeing to India

Before the war broke out, we were living in a house where the department store C. K. Tang stood. The small Tang's that was on Orchard Road 10 years ago. It was our residential address in the pre-war days. 310 Orchard Road, a wooden bungalow house on stilts.

Just before the war erupted, we moved to East Coast Road, next to a family called Bogaars. Lots of people moved to the seaside, thinking it would be safer. We felt the Japanese would attack where there was a concentration of important places, like the city area. And our residence at Orchard Road was very near the Tanglin Club, where the British officers were housed. Government House was close too. There was one important building and after one acre there was another and then another...

At the beach area, there were soldiers digging trenches. The coast was being mined. And there was barbed wire on the sea front. But right up to the day the first bombs fell, people were still dancing in the Raffles Hotel and planters were coming down to Singapore from Malaya to buy goods in Robinson's and Mark's and Spencer's. The British had such a huge empire, they thought they were gods.

Then, of course, when the Japanese sank those two ships, people realised that these little yellow people were not as the British painted them out to be — little yellow men who only sold cheap toys in Middle Road.

The night the first bombs fell, I had gone to bed to get a good night's rest after studying for my Senior Cambridge examination that was to start the next morning. The bombs were dropped in the wee hours of that morning and because of the confusion that followed, many of my friends did not turn up for the exams. They were scared. But my parents were determined that I should not miss out on school. Education was a priority for them.

As for me, I found it all pretty exciting. I was young; what did I care? The bombs were frightening because of the sound, but you were not grown-up enough to realise what damage they could do. I studied at the Anglo-Chinese School, the old building at Cairnhill Road and went to school by car. The driver had to zig zag on the road to avoid the craters caused by bombs. I remember a gaping hole in the road in front of the old Cold Storage where a bomb had exploded, but I never really saw anybody dying on the streets or anything like that. All that was cleared up by the time we went to school in the morning.

My first exam paper was Geography, I think. Two days later we had another paper, and another paper after that. We used to be bombed very regularly during the exams. If we were in school when the Japanese planes arrived on a bombing run, we quickly went down to the hall to sit and wait it out. We counted the aeroplanes. Pretty impressive sight. We had never seen so many planes.

My family had an air-raid shelter in the front garden of the house, but I don't think we ever used it. Our bigger fear was the drunken Australian soldiers whose camp was at St Patrick's School, next door to our house. Beaten, defeated fellows, who roamed around at night and... you know, may get up to something or other. They would come around to the front gate of our house and sit there all night, getting drunk and crying. They were just boys from the sheep farms of Australia. No manners; just junglies. They had lost their ideals. They must have thought how the hell could they have been beaten by these little fellas in singlets, short pants and bicycles? Guerilla warfare was started by the Japanese. They showed the British how to do it.

I kept a dagger with me because I was worried about these soldiers. Fortunately, the Indian troops, who realised that we were an Indian family residing there, would come and shoo them away. I read later that the brunt of the defence of Singapore fell on the shoulders of the Indian Army, which would have been true to form. Send the Natives out first. They are "expendable".

As the bombings continued, my mother, then pregnant, became more and more of a nervous wreck. Doctor Sloper, my mother's doctor, told my father, "Look here, you'd better send your wife away. She will not survive these bombings. You'll lose your child, as well as your wife."

So, in January 1942, my two brothers, my mother and I were put on a ship at the old Keppel wharves where Godown 44 or 45 is now. The old PNO and British passenger ships used to dock there. On the ship were a lot of other Indians. The reason the ships were there was because of my father's position as the leader of the Indian community. He was on the Governor's Executive Council. He wrote to Gandhi and the Viceroy of India for assistance as Singapore was then a colony. In reply, the British produced four ships for the Indians to evacuate to India.

Of course, it was also used as a jumping point for the British servicemen's wives and children to flee. There were quite a number of British men aboard the ship too. Many of them may have been civilians; planters leaving because their plantations had been overrun. But there were also some British men in uniform.

There weren't any Malays on the ship and only a few Chinese, the well-to-do ones. The others, poor fellows, they didn't know anybody, so how could they get on board? Whom could they turn to?

On the ship I had my first experience of what it meant to be a Native and what it meant to be a colonial ruler. I was the son of the top Indian in Singapore, right? Though I was allocated a cabin in first class, I never saw it. Instead, I was given a cabin with six people in it. And the sanitary works weren't working.

It was terrible. We had to sleep out on the deck because the cabin stank. I had two younger brothers to look after. They were twelve and nine. And my pregnant mother. So I kept my dagger with me.

All the nice cabins in first and second class were taken up by the wives of Britishers running away to sanctuary in India. These ships were not meant for them in the first place. Most of the thousand-odd Natives that were on that ship slept on deck. The open deck. When it rained, you got wet. Others slept under the deck. We were all known as deck passengers. You know the movies which show pilgrims going from Europe to America? Those were the conditions we travelled in. It really got my back up, although I was only fourteen. I was furious. And we didn't know where the ship was going either. Sure, it was going to India, but which part?

One night, the ship stopped right in the middle of the Bay of Bengal. I later learnt that a Japanese submarine had stopped the ship and the Master was told to declare himself and state who were on board.

"Oh," he said, "I've got 1,200 Indian refugees from Singapore."

So they left him alone. Otherwise they would have torpedoed the ship. There were lots of Japanese submarines in the Bay of Bengal. When my father came later, he had to change ships three times on the way to India; the first two were sunk by the Japanese.

Finally, we reached Calcutta. From there, we took a train through central India to a place called Kanpur, and then to Bombay where my mother's brother lived. And that is where I spent my days until the war ended.

The first couple of years were bad. After that, it was all right because my father was given a government job. He didn't really like it because he hadn't worked under anybody before, particularly the British. But he had little choice. I enrolled in a university, based on my Senior Cambridge results which arrived in India. I became a student leader, taking part in marches and so on because at that time India was pressing for independence.

All the evacuees who considered Singapore their home — and we did, you see — met at a club at the Taj Mahal Hotel. That's where we met the Chinese who had come from Singapore, including (Oversea-Chinese Banking Corporation chairman) Tan Chin Tuan's family.

After the war, I came home to Singapore. My father came back with Mountbatten because he was with the British Military Administration. All the Indians who had supported Subhas Chandra Bose had been put in jail here in Singapore, but my father got them all out. All except those on criminal charges.

We became a changed people. And those who had remained in Singapore also changed. Like Lee Kuan Yew. Now we understood what Japanese imperialism meant and what British imperialism meant.

I wouldn't have supported the British. I would have, in fact, supported the Japanese if they meant what they said about the Greater Asia Co-Prosperity Sphere. Get rid of the white domination. But it only meant domination by the Japanese instead. It was a replacement of masters. And a much worse and cruder people than the British, who were civilised in many ways. You could, if you reached the top, stand up and talk to them eye to eye. The Japanese, if you talked eye to eye with them, you got slapped, or punched, or kicked. Or put behind bars and tortured.

Today, the Japanese are glossing over their history. To distort it, to say, ah, that was just an incident, changing history, is not correct. It should be written as it was and the Japanese people should know what really happened. Otherwise how will they understand what we went through during the war?

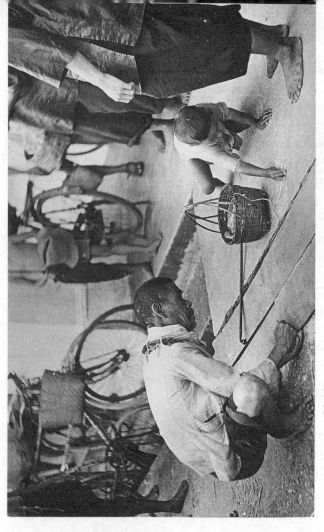

Picking up dropped grains of rice during the Occupation

> **I have flashbacks to a time when I would eat a bowl of rice to the very last grain because it was so precious.**
>
> — Author Goh Sin Tub on the food shortage during the Occupation.

Education under the Japanese

"The most profound of all means available to propaganda is education," declared the Japanese and they made the restructuring of the education system a priority.

Their ambitions were grand, but their resources limited. The unified education system they hoped for never materialised. Instead, they modified the English and vernacular language schools that were already present.

All school fees were abolished. Education became free, although hardly universal as parents were not too keen to send their children to learn a difficult tongue and learn to love an Empire that was causing them so much suffering. Children instead were more valuable at home as another resource in those difficult times.

Nonetheless, the Japanese put in much effort and by 1944, most classes in English and Chinese language schools were being conducted in Japanese. Malay schools continued teaching in Malay, which was accepted by the Japanese as an indigenous language to be encouraged. The Japanese set up a few Indian schools with unqualified teachers whose main job was to push Japanese propaganda about why the Indians should work with them to achieve Indian Independence.

Even at their peak though, all the schools put together did not draw more than 7,000 students and by

1945, as times got harder, attendance dropped to a few hundred at best.

The next few pages reveal the experience of one school during the war, St Joseph's Institution, which truly is an institution in the Singapore education landscape. The account is excerpted from the school's hardcover edition of reminiscences of old boys and past teachers, called Memories of SJI.

That story is followed by novelist Goh Sin Tub's first-hand account of life under the Japanese education system and its effect on him when he was an impressionable teenager.

St Joseph's during the war

As 1941 rolled on, there was a change in the atmosphere as more and more troops arrived on the island from India and Australia. The Catholic Club at the corner of Queen Street and Bras Basah Road was crowded with servicemen in the evenings. Air raid exercises were introduced and Civil Defence organised. Volunteer units of one kind or another were formed and a mood of apprehension gripped the city as Japan became more and more belligerent. School continued as though nothing untoward was happening.

The following account appears in the History of the House, a manuscript book kept by the Brothers:

"Meanwhile, in the atmosphere of continual preparation in case of trouble, things went on more or less normally. Trade carried on amidst the military bustle of quartering troops who were still pouring in. We handed over our fine boarding school six miles from town to the Australians, who fitted it up as a hospital. Schools functioned as usual. The final-term examinations were in the offing and beginning pupils were being registered for the year 1942, when on the morning of December 8, 1941, at four o'clock, the sleeping city of Singapore was awakened by a strange volume of sound in the air, approaching the city from the south.

267

"I was awakened from peaceful slumber and listened intently. It was the sound of a large flight of airplanes, making a noise quite distinct from the British squadrons which we had been accustomed to see and hear for months previously. I jumped out of bed, sensing that this flight of planes was something out of the ordinary and feeling that all was not well.

"Going out on the balcony, I went over to the direction from which the ever-increasing volume of low-keyed ominous droning came, and decided at once that it must be a flight of Japanese planes. I went a few steps back to an adjoining room where another Brother was awake and I asked him if they wouldn't be Jap planes. We both peered over the balcony at the huge flight (dimly outlined by a bright moon, in a sky of white, fleecy clouds), now almost over the extreme south of the sky.

"Suddenly, three or four loud explosions, accompanied by livid reddish-purple flashes, confirmed our impressions. It was my first experience of bombing. The part of the city to get the first baptism of fire was no more than half-a-mile from where we stood (gazing in awe), on the school balcony. The huge flight divided; one part going northeast, the other northwest over the city, which was ablaze with electric and gas lamps.

"They had not proceeded much further when scores of searchlight beams jumped into being, sweeping the heavens and gradually concentrating on one of the prettiest sights imaginable if the fact could be ignored that the separate groups of silver butterflies, miles up in the air, were messengers of death and destruction.

"We watched them moving along slowly and solemnly, in perfect formation, but wreathed about, above, below and on all sides — as it appeared to us — with balls of fire from scores of ack-ack shells.

"On they went, utterly ignoring the fireworks around them. They were raining down death in their apparently silent parade, as was evident from the succession of terrific explosions on the ground beneath them. They had swept over the Naval Base and the airfields, over the city and suburbs, pursued all the time by the relentless gleaming sabres which kept them in full view, and also by shell-bursts which seemed to adorn the picture without spoiling the outline. We watched breathlessly for a break in those beautifully arranged lines of silver wings. There may have been some shot down, but we saw none, to our disappointment.

"That was our first experience of bombing, as I have already stated. Luckily for us, no plane passed near our part of the city that early December morning, otherwise in the light of later experience, not one of us upon that flat roof would have had a chance of escape, had a single bomb fallen on it."

On the following day not many people were in the mood for work, but at SJI the Cambridge School Certificate Examinations were under way, under the presiding examiner, Dr Thio Chan Bee, of the Anglo-Chinese School. Everything went on as usual and when a candidate asked what he should do in the event of another air raid, he was told to carry on as if nothing unusual had occurred. Dr Thio merely wrote a brief report to the examiners in England describing the difficulties that some of the candidates were experiencing.

Meanwhile, the Japanese advanced with lightning speed down the Malayan Peninsula. The History of the House continues:

"You would find it hard to believe that school functioned for two weeks in January 1942 with the Japs at our door. It is true that only the bigger boys came. It was a matter of keeping up morale, I suppose, but at what an insane risk. Air raids were frequent and violent: no work at all was possible. We spent most of the time in interior passages splendidly arranged for mass slaughter. I had four or five days of this and could stand it no longer, so I phoned to the powers that were. I suppose that all other heads of schools felt much the same. The schools then closed until the Japs reopened them. St Joseph's was taken over as a hospital for military casualties.

"When the Royal Army Medical Corps took possession (we kept our living quarters), the first man in the first lorry which stopped under the hall portico to jump out and salute me was an Irishman from Rathdowney who had retreated the entire 550 miles from Kota Baru to Singapore with the corps intact.

"The commander was another Irishman, Colonel Malcolm, from Drogheda, beside whom my five-feet-nine inches helped little to make me look a man of average height. The Irish were thick in this fighting unit, as they proverbially are wherever there is a fight; and here I was, another Gael to welcome them and say, 'God bless you all.'

"I suggested the Map Room as the best lighted and best protected for the Operating Theatre and they fixed it up. All the forty-two classrooms became wards. The desks were piled in the corners of the verandahs and all was done amidst ceaseless bombing, shelling and machine-gunning. By now everything outside the buildings was in utter confusion. The dead lay in heaps on the streets of the city and were being buried in the fields and parks. Our front garden became a cemetery, in fact.

"Shells whined, bombs burst everywhere and were answered by anti-aircraft guns set up anywhere and everywhere. The din was appalling, the buildings trembled, the air was stifling, the heat suffocating. Hundreds and thousands of military vehicles of all descriptions choked the streets. Soldiers from all kinds of units were scattered all over the city looking frightfully woe-begone, dog-tired, crest-fallen and gloomy.

"The colonel often asked me to make the rounds with him because, as he said, 'The sight of you men of the cloth will comfort the men.' By this time I had grown fairly reckless of danger and callous to injury. I did accompany the colonel and what sights I saw on those rounds!

"The Roman Catholic chaplains were marvellous. The men wept as they watched them administer the last rites to the dying, utterly regardless of danger, for death rubbed elbows with us the whole time. A dozen or so of the poor, shell shocked soldiers cried aloud like boys when another squadron of Jap planes swept over, releasing bombs and filling the ground and walls with bullets from their machine guns.

"But the most awesome sight that ever met my gaze was the Operating Room, with surgeons amputating legs and arms to save poor soldiers who had contracted gangrene from days of exposure and lack of First Aid on the hill sides. There were the surgeons, sweating profusely, with their attendants at their elbows.

"I won't go into all the details; they are far too gruesome. I sickened at it all, could never get accustomed to the sight and smell of hot blood soaked up in bucketfuls by yards of lint and bandaging. Arms and legs were wrapped in sheeting and taken away for burial with corpses of poor fellows who died en route from the battlefield. I never liked the odour of disinfectant when going through hospitals. Here it filled what was left of the air. Oh, it was all so sad, so unnerving and so very dreadful.

"At least ten shells hit the buildings and one 500-pound bomb dropped almost in the centre of the inner courtyard."

(Ed: In an addendum, Brother Christopher Chen, wrote: It was about 4.30 pm when the bomb was dropped. At that time all the wounded Australian soldiers were lining up along the Hall, the main school building and the tuck shop where they were about to receive their evening meal. When the officer-in-charge heard the sound of a falling bomb, he blew the whistle and the soldiers at once lay flat on the ground. Another shell came through the roof right down to the classroom on the ground floor, where some officers were at that time. They were very fortunate the shell did not explode.")

The History of the House continues:

"Besides the bomb, at least ten shells hit the building. One shell cut out half the wall of a classroom in which twenty-five wounded lay. Not one of them got a scratch.

"Another shell came through the roof, right down to the ground floor without exploding. It made a hole a foot in diameter beside my desk in the Community Room on the second floor, continued down to the basement and buried itself in the ground.

"Still another cut through the walls of the (illegible) room and exploded in the courtyard. The bomb went down twenty-five feet, raised the macadamised courtyard ground around it two feet, set eight lorries on fire and cut hundreds of gashes in the walls of the buildings all around. The fire was put out with sand from sandbags. All the doors were sucked out, the fastening being torn off.

"The grandfather clock got a splinter through the pendulum, coming in on one side of the frame and going out the other side. It stopped the faithful time recorder of the past fifty years and registered the hour of Singapore's last frightful bombing to hasten the surrender in which 15,000 people were killed. The clock, for weeks afterwards, showed four-thirty exactly. That was Sunday evening, February 14, 1942."

"The numerous shells and the one bomb did not even scratch a single soul. When the dust and smoke cleared after that awful explosion and everybody, white-faced, looked at everybody else, it was found that not a single soul was hurt.

"Then followed a scene never to be forgotten. The colonel stood among the men, white-faced, shaken, but brave as a lion. I was near him. Scarcely could anybody talk. Words dried up in our throats. It was a tense moment. The colonel spoke his pleasure that nobody was hurt and looked at me appealingly. Up went two brawny arms. They were those of the chef, with his huge, tattooed chest, tousled hair, half-wild, half-sobbing face with eyes popping out of his head.

"He grabbed my hands and roared: 'Ye can thank these good men if we're alive; we're not worth it. Father, give me a rosary!'

"I gave him one. I kept several in my pocket with medals. 'I believe in God and the Christian Brothers,' he said, and he kissed the rosary and put it around his neck.

"The Brothers helped me to distribute more rosaries and medals. The Catholic boys had theirs already but now all the rest wanted them. Every man, even the rudest and roughest, has a good spot in his heart. This scene, the last before the surrender, which took place an hour after the clock stopped, might be considered the culminating point of an official mission.

"Fear and death made men search into the depths of their souls. While everything was crumbling about us in the metaphorical sense, the only thing that matters, religion, had a clear field. The human had collapsed, the Divine shone out.

"Before I pick up again the story of the battle and its consequences, I would have a few words about our shelter. We practically lived in it day and night for the last week before the fall of Singapore. The kitchen was quite near it. We lived on our reserves of tinned food and cases of aerated water with three or four bottles of good old Dublin stout.

"We were hard put to get water at all. To drink it, even after boiling, would be very dangerous. Experience showed that our foresight was wise on all counts. We risked our lives to satisfy the demands of nature; washing or bathing was out of the question. We had to live in the shelter together with forty or so sailors from the Catholic Club across the road, that was being used as a picket station.

"The 'enlightening' bomb, of which I have already made mention must be reintroduced here. It fell on the cement wall at an angle in the room in which the sailors had constructed a rude shelter of mattresses on tables reinforced by knock-down bed-frames.

"The bomb made a hole over their heads but exploded upwards and outwards. We got the benefit of the flying splinters, already recorded in detail, and the sailors got a close call too. Over they came to us, asking if we could give them a billet. We did. They looked very shaken and pale. We must have looked similar to their view.

"We became great friends and they, with the soldiers and the poor fellows, survivors of the Prince of Wales and the Repulse, stuck it out to the end. We taught many of them the rudiments of our faith at their request, the simple prayers, but above all the act of contribution, with great confidence in God. Quite a number had no religion. They drank in what we told them.

"Now let us go back to Bukit Timah. This last line was smashed by the Japs after day and night assaults. Yamashita, of evil memory, said he would reduce the city to smithereens if surrender was not forthcoming, and he ordered the demonstration massacre at Alexandra Hospital on the afternoon of the fourteenth to drive home that he meant what he said.

"The Governor, Sir Shenton Thomas, taking the advice of his military advisers, ordered the surrender of the city to prevent further slaughter in a situation recognised as hopeless. The military commanders met the Japs and formally offered unconditional surrender. It appears that they parleyed for the concession of not allowing the Jap suicide squads to enter the city. I do not know if this is true, but we were told that they were kept out.

"Of course, nobody but the authorities knew what was taking place in the last four hours, though facts came to light afterwards. We noticed, however, that the bombing had ceased, though the shelling was sporadic.

"That sad, Sunday night we were all in the shelter composing ourselves as best we could for sleep when at about 8 pm, we heard the wailing of a siren which continued for quite a long time. Then it ceased. Speculation was rife. It must be surrender. The growing quiet proved it, gave credibility to the idea. By 10 pm, there was dead silence except for a burst or so in the distance. We came out of the shelter, talked of possibilities for hours until fatigue broke up the gathering and all went to rest.

"The eclipse was total."

In the aftermath of the surrender there was universal fear and uncertainty. The streets were filled with Allied soldiers who had nowhere to go. There was some looting. Mrs de Sa's shop in Waterloo Street was looted, but St Joseph's Institution was not touched. This was because the school was taken over soon after as a temporary barracks for Japanese soldiers. And the Brothers left the air-raid shelter in the tuck shop and returned to their quarters.

Their memories of what they had been through were never to be effaced. Forty-four years afterwards, Brother Philip O'Callaghan would write:

"War experiences are very coloured things. But the rows of dead and wounded along the corridors when the school was used as a Red Cross Centre will always be tragic memories. I remember through curiosity lifting back the soiled blanket from the face of what I thought was a sleeping soldier, to find that it covered the shattered face of a nineteen-year-old Australian soldier.

"There was the afternoon, too, when I watched the orderly carrying out two bucketfuls of arms and leg stumps to bury them in the little garden in the front; and the other equally sad day when, after a shelling session, they buried the Indian soldiers killed in the football field.

"There was the day when we watched the vast army of Allied prisoners of war march into captivity after the surrender and I will always remember the cries of despair and desolation from the truckloads of young girls whisked off to the Japanese Army brothels. That was a sad scene viewed from the Waterloo Street end of the building."

In the newly named city of *Syonan*, the Japanese Military Administration appointed a municipal government which was headed by a Mayor, Shigeo Odate. This new city government parcelled out its duties between four bureaux, of which the Public Welfare Department was one.

The schools came under this bureau and, to organise education under the new dispensation, the Japanese authorities chose Mr Mamoru Shinozaki. He was a humane man, but he had had no previous connections with teaching whatsoever. He had, in fact, been interned by the British as a spy when he was a press attache at the Japanese Consulate prior to hostilities. His was one of several spy trials at the time, after which he had been shut up in Changi until he was liberated by his own people.

The new administration found itself under pressure from all sides to do something about reopening the schools. Crowds of young people were wandering about the streets, so it was primarily to restore order that Shinozaki began his work. Certain schools were designated to serve a particular locality. St Joseph's Institution was renamed the Bras Basah Boys' School and initially admitted boys from Standards VI to IX, but on May 1, 1942, it was converted into a Primary School and Brother Joseph noted that the enrolment was just 258 on that day. Senior pupils had to leave until classes for older boys were started.

The little school that now occupied the SJI building had no more identity as SJI. It was organised along ethnic lines. There were three Malay classes, two Indian classes, five Chinese classes and two mixed.

However, Brother Joseph remained as Director until December 14, 1943, when he and the other Brothers who had not been interned left Singapore. Then a Mr Jing of Raffles Institution took over the running of the school. The attendance gradually increased until 1944, but in the last year of the war it was sometimes as low as sixty-eight out of an enrolment of 233.

The curriculum of the new school consisted of singing, gymnastics, drama, handicrafts, drawing and Japanese language. Later, for urgent reasons, gardening was added.

From the first, the teaching was supposed to be conducted in Japanese. To this end, every afternoon, the teachers and Brothers had to attend a language course in which they learned the rudiments of the tongue and the outline of the lesson that they would teach their pupils the next day. Brother Philip remembers his lessons well:

"Who among the older teachers will ever forget the Japanese classes conducted in what are now the Science labs outside the chapel? The pleasant and witty Mr Hyami, the bull-like Mr Ishii, the sly little Mrs Suzuki and our charming Mrs Sakai who used to teach at St Anthony's before the war, and who came back from India after internment to teach Japanese to the teachers. Her sympathy and understanding and the fact that she knew the teachers and was such a charming lady was enough to take away our fears of the Japanese."

Teaching in the Bras Basah Boys' School was a frustrating and sometimes alarming experience. In the first place the enrolment was, at the best of times, only a quarter to half of that of pre-war SJI (1,214 in 1938). The actual attendance was lower still. Parents were fearful of sending their children. Some were afraid that their children would eventually be conscripted into the Japanese armed forces. More frequently, families felt that they needed the wages of every one of their members, including the children. Survival, not school, was their priority.

There were also frequent interruptions to the classes. The public celebration of some Japanese festival might take weeks of preparation. The first occasion was the birthday of the Japanese Emperor on April 19, 1942. All the children in the *Syonan* schools had to parade on the Padang with Japanese flags and sing the Japanese anthem. The music was sent 'round to all the schools. Lessons were abandoned for rehearsals. The help of the Police Band was enlisted and on the actual day the event passed off very successfully. The children sang to General Yamashita and the Tiger of Malaya was seen to be visibly moved.

The following day, the Director received a congratulatory message. Later, in July of the same year, the children turned out in Victoria Street to greet General Tojo when he visited *Syonan*, and the boys made 2,000 flags for the occasion.

Later still, the teachers were expected to tend vegetable plots in the Botanic Gardens. The school diary records that quite often teachers were away from 10 am to 1 pm, when school hours lasted from 9.50 am to 3 pm. Teachers also had to do night patrol duties and this necessarily meant absence from school the next day.

Initially there was an acute shortage of textbooks. In fact, Shinozaki wrote some simple language books himself. At first English was banned as a medium of instruction in the schools by the military authorities. Then Shinozaki realised that it was quite impractical to make Japanese compulsory so he went and begged Mayor Odate to have the order rescinded. This was done.

Nevertheless, the constant presence of Japanese soldiers around the corridors of SJI and the occasional visitation by be-medalled military or naval officers, who had no connection with education, made every day a nerve-wracking experience for the teachers. In fact the Brothers made the best of an impossible situation until the authorities, who had brought in a number of teachers from Japan, gradually gave them less and less to do. Finally, in November 1943, the European Brothers were told that their services were no longer required. With no job and no visible means of support, their prospects looked bleak indeed. So all the Brothers, including the local Brothers, decided to go to Bahau.

All the Brothers were in bad shape, physically, by the time the war ended. In this respect there was no difference between those who had been in the jungles of Bahau and those who had been locked up in Changi Goal. However, rest and recuperation were far from being their first consideration.

As soon as he could, the Brother Director set out for Singapore with three companions for he was afraid that the school might be looted in the interval between the end of the war and the return of the British. His premonition was correct. He found that a lot of the furniture had been used as firewood and all the electrical fittings, lamps, switches and wiring had been removed.

Even before all the Brothers had returned from Bahau the registration of new pupils had begun. About three weeks after the formal surrender of the Japanese at the Padang, the school reopened. The opening day was an extraordinary scene. The whole compound was crowded with thousands of families seeking admission for their children. The Director and ten or twelve lay masters tried to make a start. He opened eight classrooms on the first floor that was devoid of furniture and gave instructions that only former pupils were to be admitted.

In a few hours a dozen books of admission forms had been filled and then ordinary paper had to be found; this was in short supply. Hundreds of parents, whose children had never been to the Brothers' schools, had to be turned away. At St Anthony's Boys' School there were similar scenes, and also at St Patrick's, housed temporarily at Telok Kurau, where Brother Remigius was in charge.

Before they realised it, the Brothers had accepted 1,400 pupils, and they began teaching. Boxes, long boards and beaten-up tables had to do duty for chairs and desks. Army Officers, when they saw the need, supplied the school with pens, ink and paper taken from Japanese supply dumps. Little by little, school got under way, but food was in short supply, and, here again, a few army friends proved invaluable.

If the position of the Brothers was fraught with difficulty, their problems were compounded by the obtuseness of the British Military Administration. Brother Director complained that the authorities seemed never to have heard of Aided Schools, that only ceaseless agitation seemed to move them to pay the teachers a cent of salary, and that the machinery of government moved hardly at all, so bound up was it with red tape. "Thicker, redder and broader than ever before," he noted in exasperation.

The pupils had their own difficulties: many had not been inside a school since the arrival of the Japanese.

"If there had been no war," commented Lim Choo Sye, who was teaching Standard VI at SJI, "they would have been normal, respectful young fellows. But with three-and-a-half years of Japanese Occupation, of black-marketing and various kinds of activities, we had a tough job. However, in spite of having acquired bad habits like smoking and gambling, they realised that they were many years behind as far as education was concerned and so they decided to learn."

That helped the teachers, even if they were taken aback by the amount of copying that went on. "After all," commented Mr Lim, "they had no morals for three-and-a-half years."

The education authorities decreed that boys were to enter the Standard that they would have been in had there been no war. So boys who were in Standard IV in 1942 were now put in Standard VII. The consequence was that the teachers had to cover in two years the work that would normally have taken three or four years to complete.

A further consequence was gross overcrowding. Over at St Anthony's, C. R. Eber, a survivor of the notorious Burma-Siam railway, was teaching a class of seventy-five boys. Brother Ignatius, who had started teaching a class even before the official reopening, took time to teach during the holidays and on Saturday mornings. One way or another, the Brothers' schools strove to repair the damage done to a whole generation.

Meeting Goh Sin Tub

Mr Goh Sin Tub, born in 1927, is best known today as a novelist and short story writer. A smallish and bookish man, he is very alert. Despite his age, there is something very youthful about the way he looks and talks. That youthful demeanour is helped by his large, expressive Peranakan eyes.

His account gives a very good idea of what it was like to be a teenager during the war, including the emotional impact of living through such a tumultuous period at such a formative point of his life.

Mr Goh also gives a good idea of what school was like under the Japanese. His frank and honest observations of what it was like to go from a British to Japanese and back to a British education system are insightful for the way they reveal the power of any education system to inculcate life-long values.

After the war, Mr Goh became the Director of Social Welfare before he switched to a career in banking in which he achieved rapid success, rising quickly through the ranks to become Assistant General Manager of the Oversea-Chinese Banking Corporation. He was a key figure behind the construction of the OCBC Centre skyscraper that dominated the skyline in the area for years.

Mr Goh left the banking sector to join C. K. Tang

for two years before becoming the General Manager of a division of the United Overseas Bank. He retired from banking in 1986, but sits on the boards of a few companies. He was given the prestigious Public Star Award in 1989.

His lifelong interest in creative writing continues apace and his literary works include a novel and several collections of short stories.

Growing up suddenly

I was fourteen when the war broke out. It made me grow up suddenly. Before the war I had very much of a child's concerns — leading a child's life. But suddenly, at the age of fourteen, my father, who was a bank clerk at the Hongkong and Shanghai Bank, lost his job and the family had no income. My eldest brother and I did our part to support the family. I bought canned goods and sold them on the roadside. I also used to go to the bakery at Kramat Lane and buy loaves of bread that I sold door to door.

We were at 102 Emerald Hill when the bombing began. It was a two-storey shophouse with a five-foot path in front of it. It is still there. When the Japanese advanced into Singapore, they shelled Monk's Hill School because there were some British artillery units there. Monk's Hill is not far from Emerald Hill and the Japanese were not all that accurate, so some of the shells landed on Emerald Hill.

One exploded on a house just two doors away. Scared the guts out of us. That house was completely demolished. Fortunately, the residents had already fled, so nobody was killed. But the explosion was so loud, it really shook us up.

My family hid under the staircase, which we barricaded with sandbags. There was very little we could have done if there was a direct hit but if the danger was just confined to shrapnel, the sandbags protected us. And, of course, they helped to keep up the structure too. When the bombing got heavier, we decided to flee to my granduncle's house in Phillip Street. So we hastily packed a few bags — there were shells falling all around — and fled.

Somehow, we got to Phillip Street safely. My granduncle welcomed us. He was in the import-export business and he had stacks and stacks of rice and soya bean in the house, so food was not a problem. We stayed there until the bombing died down a few days later and the Japanese were in Occupation.

When the British surrendered, there were people who took advantage of the power vacuum before the Japanese moved in. They started looting. But when the Japanese soldiers moved in, they lopped off the heads of looters and exhibited them. This was a very strong deterrent because it was instant justice. I guess, if you were a victim of the looting, you would have been very thankful that the Japanese were tough on the looters.

My father and my eldest brother decided to go back to Emerald Hill to see if the house was okay. They made it there all right, but on their way back to Phillip Street, they found their path blocked by sandbags, barbed wire and Japanese soldiers. They made a dash for it, climbing over the sandbags and barbed wire. The Japanese soldiers opened fire on them, but by some miracle they managed to escape.

They came back to Phillip Street and told us that the house was okay, but we decided to wait a few more days before going back.

By then the Japanese had started their screening. All males had to report to designated places. We were told to report to a place at Tanjong Pagar Road where the old cinema, Palace Gay Theatre, stood.

There we were called out one by one and had to pass a number of people sitting at a table, both Japanese and locals. Some of those locals were traitors, pointing out people that they claimed were pro-British.

I was very scared.

They could see that I was just a kid, so they put a rubber stamp on my hand and let me through. For days after that, you didn't bathe because you didn't want the mark to fade. If you ventured into the streets and you wanted to cross the numerous barriers that had been set up, that mark was your pass.

My father too got a stamp. We were cleared. But some people were detained and my granduncle was one of them. He was the man who gave shelter to our family and many other families. There were even people whom we did not know sheltering in his house. He was a great man, a wonderful man. Very generous, willing to take anybody into his house and feed them.

He must have been fingered by some locals there. Anybody at the table could say, "Yes he is a suspect." I suppose these people were themselves roped in by the Japanese and under threat. They were identified as anti-

Japanese and asked to pick out others who were anti-Japanese. And some of them probably felt they had to pick out one out of every ten people or whatever. It was all very random. Those fingered just had very bad luck.

Later, we heard stories that those who were singled out were loaded onto trucks, taken to the seaside and shot. For months, years after that, there were rumours about what had happened to them.

There were also the vultures who would come around to my grandaunty and say, "I know something about your husband's whereabouts... we can take you to see somebody who will give you more information, but you have to pay us for the trouble."

A lot of people, blood suckers, worked this way. Capitalising on the sorrow and the fear. And this went on...

My grandaunty paid money on every occasion to try and get some news. She cried until she went blind. Literally. Her eyes were always red and they grew dim and soon she went blind. My granduncle was never found.

I found work as an apprentice in a typewriter shop at Orchard Road, where the Meridien Hotel now stands. My Japanese bosses were very understanding and friendly. They were engineers who supervised us.

I was paid a salary, which wasn't very much. But it was my first job and I was eager to learn. My Japanese bosses were impressed by my enthusiasm and introduced me to a Japanese language school at Queen Street. During the Occupation years, you had to be able to speak some

Japanese to get by. More so for me as my job was to repair Japanese typewriters.

It was not too difficult to get into the language school, especially if you had an introduction from a Japanese company. Initially there were only evening classes because most of the students were working people who were trying to pick up some Japanese. The school expanded as demand grew. The number of classes increased from one session to two sessions. Then they started morning sessions as well. And because the classes were expanding so quickly, very soon they were in need of teachers.

About a year or so after I had joined the school, although I was only a kid, they asked me to help out with the teaching. Initially I was apprehensive as I would be only a few pages ahead of my pupils. But I was to find as I went along that an excellent way to learn was to teach. When you prepared for class, you had to go through the book yourself, so you learned very fast because you had to be better than your pupils.

The method of teaching I adopted was by rote. I would point to pictures and say this is that and so on and I got the pupils to keep repeating these sentences. We used books with pictures and communicated ideas with gestures. My introduction to Chinese characters were those that appeared in the guise of Kanji, Japanese characters. You see, I spoke Hokkien at home and had no exposure to the written Chinese language. And I learnt only English at St Joseph's.

It was also the reason why I could not use Chinese

to explain the meaning of Japanese words to my predominantly Chinese pupils. My method of teaching was identical to the way I was taught by the Japanese. They spoke in Japanese and explained in Japanese; you just plunged in and went along, and eventually you got the hang of things.

One of the great things about schooling there was firstly, it was an opportunity to mix with people of your own age. It was the only action going in town for people like myself because there were no other schools. There were quite a number of older folk who attended as well, so you had a broad mix. And all of them were anxious to learn the Japanese language.

We found discipline very strict in the school. We were not used to it, having been accustomed to the relaxed style of Western education where you were encouraged to ask questions. Here, you took the cue from your teachers and accepted eveything they said. It was kind of a shock to us at the beginning. If you were late, it was a very terrible thing and if you answered back, it was worse. And you had to learn to stand to attention when you were asked to answer a question. When the teachers came into the classroom, one of the students would shout, "Ki-o-tsuke!" and all of us jumped to attention.

Every morning we had the flag-raising ceremony. We stood to attention and sang the Kimigayo, the Japanese national anthem. And bowed to the east, in the direction of the Emperor.

Apart from the language, we developed a lot of character there, partly because we were mixing with peo-

292

ple who were more mature in their outlook. You learned to distinguish between different people and perhaps benefited from the lessons of your earlier schooling life when you were taught moral principles and so on. They stood you in very good stead here because they were put to the test and you came out from that sort of situation stronger. All that we were previously taught, things like being honest, being truthful, gained a certain meaning there because you came across people whose values were not like yours and you learnt to draw the line yourself.

As for the Japanese that we came across, we thought those guys were crazy. I mean they were willing to commit *harakiri* when they didn't achieve their objective. They were so nation-conscious, they jumped rigidly to attention and so on. And they took everything so seriously. They sang *kamikaze*-type songs about how they were prepared to kill themselves for the country. They even had a special cigarette, called the Emperor's Cigarette, which their pilots smoked before they died in their *kamikaze* planes the next day. And you thought, this is ridiculous, you know. But after awhile it got to you too and you began to understand it. And you felt, hey, there's something in this. It may sound crazy, but there is a reason and some wisdom in it. Who am I to say that all of this is wrong?

Of course, there was fanaticism. But there was also a certain amount of dedication. And you grew to admire their strong patriotism because these people were living for their ideals.

Ideals seemed to matter more to our teachers, not their personal interests. And this really made you feel that there are such things as ideals, real ideals which can be cherished by adults, not just kids who latch themselves blindly to ideas.

But in the Japanese school where I was learning and later taught, I also found that for the first time I was meeting Japanese who had a different outlook on the war. Some of them were very distressed with the cruelties and tortures that were going on. Some were really ashamed of what their military was doing. They went out of their way to help the locals. They would speak up on behalf of some of the students' relatives who got into trouble with the *Kempeitai*. And some of them helped us get better jobs. A few of the teachers, who had their *ubento* — a square, wooden lunch box — delivered to them, would pass these boxes to their pupils. Some even passed their vegetable rations to me and my fellow students.

You met with that kind of kindness too, so you can't say the whole race was wrong. Of course there were a lot of cruelties, a lot of things which were wrong that were done by these people, but on the other hand, there were quite a lot of good things too.

In that process of understanding, a lot of growing up took place. And you came through that three-and-a-half years a different person. That's why I say there was a very sharp line in my personal development. Before December 1941, I was a different person. I was a kid. A child. From 1941 onwards, very quickly, I grew up.

When the Japanese left us in 1945, and we went back to school, that generation was a very different one, with a very developed sense of seriousness. We were dedicated, we felt we had a purpose in life. We wanted to do things. Some of us acquired a political bent. We decided: look, the sort of things that we were prepared to accept in the past we can no longer accept. We had pride in ourselves. Some of us ventured into commerce, government, the professions, whatever, but our attitude to life was different.

Even in little ways, our attitudes changed. For instance, during the Occupation, we learnt to appreciate what a bowl of rice meant. Today, I can still look at a bowl of rice and have a flashback to a time when I would eat it to the very last grain because it was something so precious, something to be treasured.

Those were the hungry years when you couldn't get the simplest thing like bread, for instance, because they ran out of flour. In fact, they tried to make bread from corn. And then they ran out of that as well and bread was made from soyabean. It was so hard that if you threw it on the table, it bounced off. And you ate that because there was nothing else to eat.

When the war ended, it was abrupt. I guess it was because we did not get news easily and so we were totally unaware of developments elsewhere. We had heard rumours that the Japanese were losing the war. And, in fact, we heard from some of our Japanese friends, those teachers I mentioned earlier, that things were not going so well for the Japanese. But it was still a shock because we thought that as the Japanese had occupied Malaya all the way down to Singapore, they were entrenched. But all of a sudden those bombs that were dropped on Hiroshima and Nagasaki did the trick and the Japanese surrendered.

There were mixed reactions. First, I felt, well, it's a good thing that all the terror and fear was gone. You see, although we were mainly with Japanese people who were quite kind, you still heard stories of brutality and you saw the *Kempeitai* strutting through the streets. Sometimes you saw things that were unfair and cruel. And you could do nothing about it. Things like people taken away by the Japanese for listening to the radio.

You were living from day to day, never really knowing what was going to happen next. You had your routine of school or work, but you were always waiting for the unexpected. When any member of the family didn't come home or came home late, you were really worried. There was nobody you could turn to. Sure, there were the police, but they were under the Japanese. In fact, if something happened and the *Kempeitai* were involved, you had no hope.

So you were glad in a way that all that was gone.

But you were sad in a sense because some of the friends that you had made were dispersing. You were also uncertain about the future if you already had part of your future planned. For example, I was starting off a career in teaching. And now I had no idea what would become of it.

And perhaps some of the Japanese ideas about the Co-prosperity Sphere, that they were creating a new empire, were sinking in and you felt a part of that. Some of the culture and values were seeping into you because you were at a very impressionable age. The sense that your country, your civilisation, your society, should come first. That the individual should be suppressed. That you should contribute to the improvement of the whole society.

The Japanese were talking about Asia being for the Asians, and *Hikari Wa Toho Yori*, that the light comes from the East. You had a feeling that something was evolving and you were a part of it.

But all of a sudden, it was all gone, you see. And you felt a sense of loss. Which direction to take now? You couldn't go back to your childhood. You couldn't go back to the British situation. Where could you go? You submitted yourself back to parental control.

My parents said go back to school. And I did. But you went back to school very serious, very mature. You felt you had to make your mark. Go through school. Go to university. My parents couldn't afford to send me to university, so I had to work very hard to make sure I got a scholarship to get in. Which I did.

The British style of government was more liberal in the sense that you did not go about in fear. But I suppose if you had the wrong ideas and you were labelled an enemy, you would be living in fear under the British too.

For example, when I went to the university, some

of my peers were people who were very political and they got into trouble. And you began to feel that although there was a certain amount of liberty to express yourself, there were limits. And we were not prepared to accept limits anymore.

Before the war, you regarded the British, the white man, as a superior race. I know that my father's attitude to the white man was different from mine. And my children's attitude is totally different from mine too. My children would accept them or reject them as no worse or no better than themselves. For me, at one time I regarded them as better than me. The Japanese changed all that because you saw that white men were not supermen.

And then after the war, it was a different approach altogether. There was a certain degree of hostility towards them because you realised they were trying to keep you down. And you were no longer prepared to accept being kept down.

I was working in the Civil Service at that time and I felt that we could do things ourselves. And they were saying, "Look, you people are not ready to govern yourselves. You just do not know how to do it."

And we told them they were talking rubbish. They were not supermen. We knew that. The Japanese Occupation, in a way, had proved it to us. To some extent, the Japanese Occupation was a great eye-opener. And I think that was the beginning of change. Of course the generation after us did not have this queer perception of what the white man was. When they grew up, we were already independent. So it was a different thing entirely for them.

But I don't see the Occupation as an entirely dark period. I can recognise that there were black patches, but I can see some glorious red and white. I can see some technicolour.

Some experiences from that period inculcated me with certain values and a determination in life. Phrases stick in my mind, for example, the Japanese phrase, "*Gambare*!" which means hang in there, just accept it, take it and see it through. That spirit still infuses me.

And then there are snatches of Japanese songs that you learnt as a kid that come to mind from time to time. You may feel the spirit of the song. The heroic effort, the stoicism that can make you superhuman. And you can call it up in yourself, it is something in-built, you can invoke it because it's really become a part of you.

I believe that everyone has the capacity to draw good things from his environment, no matter how bad the environment may be. It's a state of mind. Look at those POWs in Changi Prison in such wretched conditions who nonetheless helped their fellow human beings.

Beauty and heroism are not where you find it. You draw it out of yourself. It is not situations that make you good or bad. It is you.

Books consulted

Singapore 1941-1942, The Japanese Version of the Malayan Campaign of World War II, by Masanobu Tsuji
(Oxford University Press, 1988)
History of the Second World War, by Liddell Hart
(Pan Books, 1973)
The Knights of Bushido, A Short History of Japanese War Crimes, by Lord Russell of Liverpool (Trinity Press, 1958)
Red Star Over Malaya, Resistance and Social Conflict During And After The Japanese Occupation 1941-1946, by Cheah Boon Kheng (Singapore University Press, 1983)
Tan Kah-kee, The Making of an Overseas Chinese legend, by C. F. Yong (Oxford University Press, 1987)
The Second World War, Vol 1 **The Gathering Storm**, by Winston Churchill (Houghton Mifflin, 1948)
— Vol 2 **The Finest Hour** (Houghton Mifflin, 1949)
— Vol 3 **The Grand Alliance** (Houghton Mifflin, 1950)
— Vol 4 **The Hinge of Fate** (Houghton Mifflin, 1950)
The Worst Disaster, The Fall of Singapore, by Professor Raymond Callahan (University of Delaware Press, 1977)
The Japanese Files, by Eric Robertson (Heinemann Asia, 1986)
Shenton of Singapore, Governor and Prisoner of War, by Brian Montgomery (Times Books International, 1984)
The History of the Jews In Singapore 1830-1945, by Eze Nathan (Herbilu Editorial & Marketing Services, 1986)
The Fall of Singapore, by Timothy Hall
(Mandarin, Australia 1990)

Recollections, Chinese Jetsam on a Tropic Shore, When Singapore was Syonan-to, by N. I. Low (Eastern University Press, 1983)

Pacific Victory, A Short History of Australia's Part in the War against Japan, by Hugh Buggy (Issued under the direction of the Australian Minister of Information, A. A. Calwell)

The Naked Island, True Stories of World War II, by Russell Braddon (Pan Books 1958)

Above And Beyond, The Full Sweep of Our Pacific Air War from Pearl Harbour to Tokyo, by Wilbur H. Morrison (Bantam Books, 1986)

Sinister Twilight, The Fall of Singapore, by Noel Barber (Arrow Books, 1968)

Memories of SJI, Reminiscences of Old Boys and Past Teachers of St Joseph's Institution, Singapore (St Joseph's Institution, 1987)

When Singapore Fell, by Joseph Kennedy (The Macmillan Press, 1989)

Malaya Upside Down, by Chin Kee Onn (Federal Publications, 1976)

And The Dawn Came Up Like Thunder, by Leo Rawlings (Eastern University Press, 1985)

British Rule In Malaya 1942-1957, by Robert Heussler (Heinemann Asia, 1985)

The Double Tenth Trial, by Sleeman, Colin & Silkin, S. C. (Wm. Hodge, 1951)

Intisari, The Research Journal of Wider Malaysia, Vol. IV, No. 1, November, 1973

Freedom In Internment, Under Japanese Rule In Singapore 1942-1945, by Tyler Thompson (Kefford Press, undated)

Mopping Up Operation, Singapore 1942-45, Oral History Department tape, 1986

A Battle To Be Remembered, Oral History Department, 1988

Japan Past And Present, by Edwin O. Reischauer (Alfed A. Knopf, 1972)

Medical History Of The War In Malaya, by R. B. MacGregor, CMC, The Medical Journal of Malaya, Vol. 3. No. 3, March, 1949.

Why Singapore Fell, by Lt-Gen Gordon Bennett (Thacker, 1945)

The Singapore Story, by K. Attiwill (Muller, 1959)

The War Against Japan, Major-Gen. Kirby Woodburn, (HMSO, 1957)